LEONARDO DA VINCI

Artist, Thinker and Man of Science

Text: Eugène Müntz (extracts)

Layout:
Baseline Co Ltd
61A-63A Vo Van Tan Street
District 3, Ho Chi Minh City
Vietnam

© 2010, Sirrocco, London, UK
© 2010, Confidential Concepts, Worldwide, USA

All rights reserved

No part of this publication may be reproduced or adapted without the permission of the copyright holder, throughout the world. Unless otherwise specified, copyrights on the works reproduced lies with the respective photographers. Despite intensive research, it has not always been possible to establish copyright ownership. Where this is the case, we would appreciate notification.

ISBN: 978-1-84484-455-5
Printed in Indonesia

Publisher's Note

Out of respect for the author's original work, this text has not been updated, particularly regarding changes to the attribution and dates of the works, which have been and are still at times, uncertain.

EUGÈNE MÜNTZ

LEONARDO DA VINCI

Artist, Thinker and Man of Science

CONTENTS

I. LEONARDO'S CHILDHOOD AND HIS FIRST WORKS

T he artist Leonardo da Vinci embodies both modern intellect and the combination of superior expression in art and science: a thinker, a poet and a wizard, Leonardo da Vinci is an artist whose fascination is still unrivalled today.

While studying his art in its incomparable variety, we find in his very caprices, to use Edgar Quinet's motto with a slight modification, "the laws of the Italian Renaissance and the geometry of universal beauty".

Outside of the small number of his finished compositions: *The Virgin of the Rocks, The Last Supper, Saint Anne,* and the *Mona Lisa,* his painted and sculpted works were left to us in marvellous fragments. We must turn to his drawings to understand all the tenderness of his heart and all the wealth of his imagination. Two specific periods of human life fixed Leonardo's attention: adolescence and old age; childhood and maturity had less interest for him. He has left us a whole series of adolescent types, some dreamy, some ardent.

In modern art, I can think of no creations so free, superb, spontaneous, in a word, divine, to oppose to the marvels of antiquity. Thanks to Leonardo's genius these winged diaphanous figures evoke a desire to be transported to this region of perfection.

When he depicted maturity, Leonardo displayed vigour, energy, and an implacable determination; men resembling an oak tree like the figure shown in their solid carved form at the Windsor Library. This drawing is comparable with another drawing where the personage is younger.

Old age passes before us in all its diverse aspects of majesty or decrepitude. Some faces are reduced to the mere bony substructure while in others we note the deterioration of specific features such as the hooked nose, the chin drawn up to the mouth, the relaxed muscles or a balding head. Foremost among these examples is the master's self-portrait which portrays a powerful head with piercing eyes under puckered eyelids, a mocking mouth, an almost bitter in expression, a delicate, well-proportioned nose, long hair and a long disordered beard which resembles that of a magician.

If we turn to his evocations of the feminine ideal we will meet a freshness and variety of style. His women were candid and enigmatic as well as proud and tender, their eyes misty with languor, or their brilliant with indefinable smiles. Yet, similar to Donatello, he was one of those exceptionally great artists who lived a life where woman did not play an important role. While Eros showered his arrows all around the master in the epicurean world of the Renaissance; while Giorgione and Raphael died victims of passions too fervently reciprocated; while Andrea del Sarto sacrificed his honour for the love of his capricious wife, Lucrezia Fedi; while Michelangelo, the sombre misanthrope, cherished an affection no less ardent than respectful for Vittoria Colonna, Leonardo, in contrast, consecrated himself without reserve to art and science and soared above all human weaknesses, the delights of the mind sufficing him. He proclaimed it in plain terms: "Fair humanity passes, but art endures" (*Cosa bella mortal passa e non arte*).

Painter and sculptor, Leonardo was also an incredibly accomplished poet. He is, indeed, pre-eminently a poet; first of all, in his pictures, which evoke a whole world of delicious impressions; and secondly, in his prose, notably in his *Trattato della Pittura,* which has only lately been given to the world in its integrity.

The thinker and the moralist are both allied to the poet. Leonardo's aphorisms and maxims form a veritable treasury of Italian wisdom at the time of the Renaissance. They offer an evangelic gentleness and an infinite sweetness and serenity.

The man of science, in his turn, demands our homage. It is not a secret to anyone that Leonardo was a *savant* of the highest order. He discovered twenty laws, a single one of which

Bust of a Young Woman, 1452-1519. Drawing with red chalk on paper. Galleria dell'Accademia, Venice.

has sufficed for the glory of his successors. He invented the very method of modern science. The names of certain men of genius, Archimedes, Christopher Columbus, Copernicus, Galileo, Harvey, Pascal, Newton, Lavoisier and Cuvier are associated with discoveries of greater renown. Nevertheless, is there another who united such a multitude of innate gifts, who brought a curiosity so passionate, an ardour so penetrating to bear on such various branches of knowledge? Or who had such illuminating flashes of genius and such an intuition of the unknown links connecting things capable of being harmonized?

In this brief sketch, we have some of the traits that made Leonardo the equal of Michelangelo and Raphael as one of the sovereign masters of sentiment, thought and beauty.

It is necessary to commence this dialogue at the beginning of the master's artistic life. The painter of the *Last Supper* and the *Mona Lisa,* the sculptor of the equestrian statue of Francesco Sforza, the scientific genius who foresaw so many of our modern discoveries and inventions was born in 1452 in the town called Empoli, on the right bank of the Arno, between Florence and Pisa. The little town of Vinci, in which he first saw the light, lies hidden away among the multitudinous folds of Monte Albano.

Certain biographers describe the castle in which Leonardo first saw the light. They conjured up a tutor who was attached to the family and a library where the child first found food for his burning curiosities. All this is legend and not based on actual fact though there actually was a castle in Vinci, but it was a fortress and a stronghold held by Florence. As for Leonardo's parents, we only know that they lived in a very modest house, but we do not even know for certain if this house was situated within the walls of Vinci itself or beyond it in the village of Anchiano.

Their domestic help consisted of one *fante,* a woman servant, at a wage of eight florins per annum.

His father, Ser Piero, was twenty-two or twenty-three years old at the time of Leonardo's birth. He was, according to recent documentation, an active, intelligent and enterprising man, and the true supporter of the family. Beginning with very little, his practice rapidly grew and he acquired a large amount of property and land.

While still very young, Ser Piero formed a relationship with the woman who, though never his wife, became the mother of his eldest son. Her name was Catarina and in all probability a simple peasant girl from Vinci or its vicinities. (An anonymous writer of the sixteenth century confirms that Leonardo was *"per madre nato di bon sangue."*)It was a short romance. Ser Piero married in the year of Leonardo's birth, while Catarina married a man of her own standing who answered to the name of Chartabrigha or Accartabrigha di Piero del Vaccha, most likely a peasant as well because of the lack of work available in Vinci. Contrary to modern customs and traditional code, Ser Piero took care of the rearing of his child.

Leonardo da Vinci united physical beauty and infinite grace in all his actions and as for his talent, no matter what difficulty presented itself, he solved it without effort. In him dexterity was allied to exceeding great strength; his spirit and his courage showed something kingly and magnanimous.

Finally, his reputation became so widespread during his lifetime that it has extended into today. Vasari, to whom we owe this eloquent appreciation, concludes with a phrase untranslatable in its power of rendering the majesty of the person described: *"Lo splendor dell' aria sua, che bellissimo era, rissereneva ogni animo mesto"* (the splendour of his aspect, which was beautiful beyond measure, rejoiced the most sorrowful souls).

Leonardo was naturally gifted with unusually muscular strength. He could twist the clapper of a bell or a horseshoe as if it were made of lead. Along with his unnatural strength came certain weakness that was mingled with this extraordinary aptitude. The artist was left-handed and in his old age paralysis finally deprived him of the use of his right hand.

From the very beginning – according to Vasari's testimony – the child showed an immoderate and at times even extravagant thirst for knowledge of any kind. He would have made even more extraordinary progress had it not been for his marked instability of purpose.

Leonardo da Vinci and **Andrea del Verrocchio,**

The Madonna with the Child and Angels, c. 1470.

Tempera on wood panel,

96.5 x 70.5 cm.

The National Gallery, London.

He threw himself ardently into the study of one science after another and bounded to the very root of questions, but abandoned work as readily as he began it. During the few months he devoted himself to mathematics, he acquired such knowledge of the subject that he confused his master all the time and put him to shame. He was also very musical. He excelled particularly on the lute, the instrument he used later for the accompaniment of the songs he improvised. In short, like another Faust, he desired to cross the vast cycle of human knowledge and, not content to have assimilated the discoveries of his contemporaries, to address himself directly to nature in order to extend the field of science.

Leonardo's father is assumed to have resided in Florence more often than in Vinci and it was undoubtedly in the illustrious capital of Tuscany, not in the obscure little town of Vinci, that the brilliant faculties of the child progressed and developed. It has been discovered that the site where the house that was once occupied by the family stood in the *Piazza* in San Firenze where the Gondi palace now stands. Apparently their home disappeared towards the end of the fifteenth century when Giuliano Gondi pulled it down to make room for the palace to which he gave his name.

According to the story, Ser Piero da Vinci was inspired by the marked aptitude of his son and took some of his sketches to his friend Verrocchio who he begged to give his opinion. They made an excellent impression and Verrocchio did not hesitate to accept the youth as his pupil.

As seen elsewhere, the majority of the artists of the Renaissance were distinguished by their precocity. Andrea del Sarto began his apprenticeship at seven years old; Perugino at nine; Fra Bartolommeo at ten; at fifteen Michelangelo executed the mask of a satyr that attracted the notice of Lorenzo the Magnificent. Finally, Mantegna painted his first masterpiece – the *Madonna of the Church of St Sophia at Padua* – when he was seventeen.

Andrea Verrocchio (born 1435) was only seventeen years older than his pupil, an advantage that seemed relatively slight over such a precocious genius as Leonardo. We may add that the worthy Florentine sculptor developed very slowly and had long been absorbed with goldsmith's work and other tasks of a secondary character. Notwithstanding the grand scale of his growing taste for sculpture, he took to the last those decorative works that were the delight of his contemporaries, the Majani, the Civitali and the Ferrucci. We learned from a document from 1488 that up until the very eve of his death he was engaged working on a marble fountain for King Mathias Corvinus. From therein he proves himself to be a true quattrocentist.

The famous art critic Rio, spoke of the natural sympathy between Verrocchio and Leonardo stating that:

"in neither artist does harmony exclude force; they show the same admiration for the masterpieces of Greek and Roman antiquity, the same predominance of the plastic qualities, the same passion for finish of details in great as well as small compositions, the same respect for perspective and geometry in their connection with painting, the same pronounced taste for music, the same tendency to leave a work unfinished and begin a fresh one and, more remarkable still, the same predilection for the war-horse, the monumental horse and all the studies appertaining thereto."

However, these points of contact could be due more to chance rather than any intellectual relationship between the two temperaments? Verrocchio had a limited spirit, a prosaic character while Leonardo, on the other hand, was the personification of unquenchable curiosity, of aristocratic tastes, of innate grace and elegance. One raises himself laboriously towards a higher ideal while the other brings that ideal with him into the world.

Under this master Leonardo was thrown in with several fellow-students who, though without attaining his glory, also achieved a brilliant place among painters. The first of these was Perugino.

Drapery Study for a Sitting Figure, c. 1470.
Pen, grey tempera and white highlights, 26.6 x 23.3 cm.
Musée du Louvre, Paris.

Workshop of **Andrea del Verrocchio**, *Study of the Angel of The Baptism of Christ*, c. 1470. Metalpoint and ochre, 23 x 17 cm. Biblioteca Reale, Turin.

Leonardo da Vinci and **Andrea del Verrocchio**, *The Baptism of Christ*, 1470-1476. Oil and tempera on wood panel, 177 x 151 cm. Galleria degli Uffizi, Florence.

Leonardo da Vinci and **Andrea del Verrocchio**, *The Baptism of Christ* (detail), 1470-1476. Oil and tempera on wood panel, 177 x 151 cm. Galleria degli Uffizi, Florence.

It is possible that Leonardo may have also met another artist, much his senior, in Verrocchio's studio, where he was working rather as an assistant than a pupil – Sandro Botticelli.

Taking into consideration Leonardo's facetious humour, his delight in mystification and his extravagant habits, it is highly probable that he formed close relationships with a band of hare-brained young fellows who frequented Verrocchio's studio whose wild doings often scandalized the good citizens of Florence and formed the characteristic traits of Florentine manners. If in the Umbrian schools, the embryo painter (such as Raphael) had all the gentleness and timidity of a young girl while in Florence, during Giotto's time, practical joking never ceased to form an integral part of the education of an artist.

Leonardo soon abandoned the common practice of studying fabric from models. In the *Trattato della Pittura* he strongly advises students not to make use of models over which paper or thin leather has been drawn but, on the contrary, to sketch their draperies from nature, carefully noting differences of texture.

However rebellious Leonardo may have been to contemporary influences, it was impossible that there should have been no interchange of ideas and no affinity of style between him and his master. To make them better understood, I will compare the various stages in the development of Verrocchio's art, as I have endeavoured to define them, with some of the more salient landmarks in the evolution of his immortal pupil.

We do not know for certain when he entered Verrocchio's studio, but it was long before 1472, at that time being only twenty years of age, he was received into the guild of painters of Florence.

Should I be accused of temerity if, armed with these dates, I venture to maintain, contrary to common opinion, that between pupil and master there was an interchange of ideas particularly advantageous to the latter; that Leonardo gave to Verrocchio as much, if not more, than he received from him? By the time that the fragrance of grace and beauty began to breathe from Verrocchio's work, Leonardo was no longer an apprentice, but a consummate master. The *Baptism of Christ* is not the only work in which the collaboration of the two artists is palpable and the contrast between the two manners self-evident; this contrast is still more striking between the works of Verrocchio made prior to Leonardo's entry into his studio and those he produced later.

Vasari tells us that after having seen the kneeling angel at the side of the Christ painted by Leonardo, Verrocchio, in despair, threw down his brushes and gave up painting.

A careful study of the picture confirms the probability of this story. Nothing could be more unsatisfactory, more meagre, than the two chief figures, Christ and St John; without distinction of form, or poetry of expression, they are simply laborious studies of some aged and unlovely model, some wretched mechanic whom Verrocchio got to pose for him. Charles Perkins justly criticizes the hardness of the lines, the stiffness of the style and the absence of all sentiment.

On the other hand look at the consummate youthful grace of the angelic tradition that was assigned to Leonardo! How the lion reveals himself with the first stroke of his paw and for what excellent reason did Verrocchio confess himself vanquished! It is not impossible that the background was also the work of the young beginner; it is a fantastic landscape, not unlike that of the *Mona Lisa*. The brown scale of colour, too, resembles that which Leonardo adopted, notably in the *Saint Jerome,* of the Vatican Gallery, in the *Adoration of the Magi* of the Uffizi (which, however, is only a sketch), in the *Virgin of the Rocks* and in the *Mona Lisa.*

In conclusion, Leonardo never dreamt, and for excellent reason, of looking to Verrocchio for ready-made formulae like those by which Raphael profited so long in Perugino's studio. It was rather he who opened up to his astonished master unsuspected sources of beauty, which the latter scarcely had time to turn to account.

Yet a contract was established between the two artists and it is with good reason that their names are inseparable in the history of art. If Leonardo played his part in his master's progress, as demonstrated by the superior inspiration behind his later works, then the patient, laborious, obstinate Verrocchio taught him to think and to search - no small task. At the same

Drapery for a Kneeling Figure,
c. 1475. Brush, grey tempera and
white highlights, 28.8 x 15 cm.
The Barbara Piasecka Collection,
Monaco.

time the goldsmith, master of perspective, sculptor, engraver, painter and musician, this eminently curious spirit must have broadened and opened his pupil's mind to varied horizons as the scattering of his talents was then the greatest danger to threaten the young Leonardo.

At the beginning of Leonardo's career, like every great artist, we meet with the legend and his first masterpiece.

"A farmer," so the story goes, "asked Ser Piero da Vinci to get a shield that he had made out of the wood of a fig tree on his property in Florence. Ser Piero demanded his son to paint something on it, but without telling him where it came from. Thinking that the shield was warped and very roughly cut, Leonardo straightened it out by heat and sent it to a turner to plane and polish. After giving it a coating of plaster and arranging it to his satisfaction, he thought of a suitable subject to painting upon it – something that comes from nature to strike terror in anyone who might attack the owner of the piece of armour, after the manner of the Gorgon of old. From then on he collected, in a place to which he alone had access, a number of crickets, grasshoppers, bats, serpents, lizards and other strange creatures; by mingling these together he evolved a most horrible and terrifying monster, whose noisome breath filled the air with flames as it issued from a rift among gloomy rocks, black venom streaming from its open jaws, its eyes darting fire, its nostrils belching forth smoke. The young artist suffered severely from the stench arising from all these dead animals, but his ardour enabled him to endure it bravely to the end. The work was completed and neither his father nor the peasant coming to claim the shield, Leonardo reminded his father to have it removed. Ser Piero, therefore, came one morning to the room occupied by his son and knocked at the door; it was opened by Leonardo, who begged him to wait a moment before entering. The young man placed the shield on an easel in the window and arranged the curtains so that the light fell upon the painting in dazzling brilliancy. Ser Piero, forgetting the errand upon which he had come, experienced at the first glance a violent shock, never thinking that this was anything but a shield and, still less, that he was looking at a painting. He fell stepped back in alarm, but Leonardo restrained him. 'I see, father,' he said, 'that this picture produces the effect I hoped for; take it, then and convey it to its owner.' Ser Piero was greatly amazed and lauded the strange device adopted by his son. He then went secretly and purchased another shield, ornamented with a heart pierced by an arrow and this he gave to the peasant who doubtfully ever after regarded him with gratitude. Afterwards, Ser Piero sold Leonardo's shield secretly to some merchants of Florence for 100 ducats and they, in their turn, easily obtained 300 for it from the Duke of Milan."

This picture was long identified with the one in the Uffizi. However, the art oracles decided that it could not have been produced until long after the death of da Vinci and that it is the work of a cinquecentist who painted it from Vasari's description. We know, however, from the testimony of an anonymous biographer that a *Medusa* that was painted by Leonardo was included in the collections of Cosimo de' Medici around the middle of the sixteenth century. Cosimo's inventory is not very precise; it mentions "*un quadro con una Furia infernale del Vinci semplice.*"

The cartoon of *The Fall* has shared the fate of the *Medusa*. Here again we have to be content with Vasari's description, corroborated by the testimony of the biographer edited by Milanesi.

Thus, from his early youth, Leonardo showed a taste for bizarre subjects: the monster painted on the shield, the Gorgon surrounded with serpents, so little in harmony with the prevailing taste of contemporary Italian artists, which was becoming more and more literary. Thus, in *The Fall*, he was engaged upon the reproduction of the very smallest details of vegetation. His burning curiosity searched into problems of the most intricate, not to say repulsive order.

Modern criticism, inconsolable at the loss of these early masterpieces, has ingeniously endeavoured to fill up a gap in Leonardo's work by a series of productions which undoubtedly reveal the influence of the young artist, but which have been too hastily accepted as his own.

One of the earliest and most interesting among these is the *Annunciation* in the Louvre, in the gallery overlooking the river. This picture, which is of very small dimensions (16 cm high by 60 cm wide), was formerly arched at the top but is now rectangular. It was attributed to Lorenzo di Credi until Bayersdorfer, whose opinion was adopted by Morelli, proposed to give it the name of Leonardo. The curly-headed angel kneeling in a sort of ecstasy in front of the Virgin refers to the one in the *Annunciation* of the Uffizi. The Virgin, too, represents the Leonardesque type, with an added touch of *morbidezza*. This type was adopted by Boltraffio and many other Milanese pupils of the master. Although the impasto is very thick, the accessories – the desk in front of which the Virgin is seated and the seats near it – are rendered with infinite care. The little piece of landscape in the background is beautiful, tranquil and imposing. The trees, unfortunately, have blackened.

The *Annunciation* of the Louvre differs from that of the Uffizi firstly in its dimensions, its narrowness being quite abnormal and secondly, in the attitude of the Virgin, who is seen here in profile, while in the Uffizi picture she faces three-quarters to the front. This Virgin has been compared with a study of a head in the Uffizi. Another head, three-quarters face, in the library at Windsor, is also akin. On the other hand, the angel of the Louvre suggests that of the Uffizi in every way. The attitude is identical; he kneels on one knee, the right hand raised, the left falling to the level of the knee.

In spite of the charm of the composition, we may be permitted to hesitate as to its authenticity for various reasons. The *Annunciation* has a precision, a rigor and firmness of outline which is rarely found in the authentic works of Leonardo. He normally banished architecture as much as possible from his compositions (his only exception to this rule being

The Annunciation, 1472-1475.
Oil on wood panel, 98 x 217 cm.
Galleria degli Uffizi, Florence.

his *Last Supper)*, in order to leave a wider field for landscape and aerial perspective. The presence of the magnificent classical pedestal, which serves the Virgin for a reading desk, is also inspires some doubt. Would Leonardo, who rarely copied Greek or Roman sculptures, have been likely to reproduce this with such elaboration?

Following the two *Annunciations,* Leonardo creates a *Virgin and Child*, acquired in 1889 by the Munich Pinacothek and now known under the title of the *Virgin with the Carnation*. The history of this small painting (40 x 60 cm) is quite a romance! Sold at Günzburg for the modest sum of one guinea it was bought again almost immediately by the Pinacothek and instantly declared to be a masterpiece. It is a most enthralling work, combining a grand and dignified solemnity with extreme finish and consummate modelling; a penetrating poetic charm breathes from the picture. Even if the puffy cheeked rendition of the Child resembles somewhat too closely the rather unsympathetic type created by Lorenzo di Credi, the Virgin captivates us with the grace of her features and the elegance of her costume: a pale blue dress with very complicated modulations, a red bodice and sleeves and a yellow scarf falling over the right shoulder and on to the knees. This example is vaporous like many of da Vinci's works. The impasto is rich in flesh tones (particularly those of the Child), which incline to blue.

According to Vasari, our sole guide for this period of the master's life, Leonardo worked on sculpture as well as painting. At the same time he studied architecture, sketching out plans of buildings that were more picturesque than practical and lastly applied himself with ardour to study the question that he had a passion all his life, the movement of water. It was then that he drew up a project for the canalization of the Arno between Florence and Pisa.

During his first efforts as a sculptor, Leonardo executed busts of smiling women and children that were worthy of a finished artist. A bust dating from this period, *Christ,* was later

Portrait of a Young Girl,
Ginevra de' Benci, 1474-1476.
Oil on wood panel, 38.1 x 37 cm.
The National Gallery of Art,
Washington, D.C.

The Madonna of the Carnation,
c. 1470.
Oil on wood panel, 62 x 47.5 cm.
Alte Pinakothek, Munich.

22

in the possession of the Milanese painter-author, Lomazzo, who describes it as marked by a child-like simplicity and candour, combined with an expression of wisdom, intelligence and truly divine majesty.

We now know the models that inspired the young da Vinci; these were modelled after the productions of Verrocchio, the polychrome terracotta of the della Robbia. In the *Trattato della Pittura* he makes special mention of them though only in reference to their technique.

After 1478, we feel we are at last on firm ground. A drawing in the Uffizi, which Charles Ravaisson-Mollien called attention to inform us with some valuable indications bearing upon Leonardo's work after he left Verrocchio. This drawing, inscribed with the date in question, shows us that by this time period the young master had already decided to study of these character-heads, beautiful or not, which were destined to occupy a very large place in his work. He sketched the portrait of a man about sixty, with a hooked nose, a bold and prominent chin, a very forcibly modelled throat; the expression is energetic and the whole composition as free as it is assured. All trace of archaism has disappeared; the flexibility of the treatment is extraordinary; the supreme difficulties in the interpretation of the human countenance are triumphantly surmounted. The sketch of 1478, somewhat softened, became a marvellous study in red chalk which is also in the Uffizi. Opposite this head, which attracts all eyes, is the head of a young man, very lightly sketched, with flowing languorous lines that are the very essence of Leonardo's art. There are also sketches of mill wheels and something like an embryo turbine – the complete Leonardo already revealed. "On the... 1478, I began the two Virgins" is written above the drawing. We do not know who these two Madonnas were and their identity opens up a wide field for conjecture.

By this time, Leonardo's fellow citizens and even the government had begun to take note of his fame. On Januray 1st, 1478, the Signory of Florence commissioned him to paint an altarpiece for the chapel of St Bernard in the Palazzo Vecchio in the courtyard of Piero del Pollajuolo. The fate of this work was, alas, like that of so many others. Having thrown himself with ardour into the task (on the 16th March the same year he received 25 florins on account) the artist tired of it and the Signory was obliged, on 20 May 1483, to apply, first to Domenico Ghirlandajo and subsequently to Filippino Lippi, who carried out the commission in 1484. His picture, however, was not placed in the chapel of St Bernard but in the Hall of Lilies in the Palazzo Vecchio. Müller-Walde identifies the picture left unfinished by Leonardo with the *Adoration of the Magi* in the Uffizi, in which other critics see the cartoon designed for the convent of San Donato at Scopeto. The *Cicerone* believes it may have been the *St Jerome* in the Vatican.

Leonardo's thirtieth birthday was approaching and he was working on his own account. His reputation was then so established that in March 1481 the monks of the rich monastery of San Donato at Scopeto, beyond the Porta Romana, commissioned him to paint the altarpiece for their high altar, *la Pala per l'Altare Maggiore*.

The artist began working at once but, again yielding to his fatal tendency, he soon put the unfinished work aside. The monks waited patiently for about fifteen years. At last, in despair, they addressed themselves to Filippino Lippi. In 1496, more expeditious than Leonardo, he delivered the beautiful *Adoration of the Magi,* the brilliant and animated work that now hangs in the same room with Leonardo's unfinished painting in the Uffizi.

However, there are several objections to this argument. The interval between Leonardo's commission (1481) and Filippino's (about 1496) is so great that the friars may very well have changed their minds and chosen a new subject. On the other hand, it is possible that Leonardo may have treated the same subject twice which is more likely.

In June 1481, the picture ordered by the monks of San Donate was so far advanced that the brothers made a purchase of ultramarine, a precious substance only used for definitive paintings. However, the Uffizi cartoon is simply a sketch in bistre. A further objection is that one of the studies for the *Adoration of the Magi* appears on the back of a sketch for Leonardo's masterpiece, the *Last Supper*. This juxtaposition is difficult to explain if the cartoon

The Madonna with a Flower (The Madonna Benois), 1475-1478. Oil on canvas transferred from wood, 49.5 x 33 cm. The State Hermitage Museum, St. Petersburg.

was really painted in 1481, some ten years before the fresco. Finally, the style of the cartoon is akin, in parts, to that of Leonardo's works of 1500 rather than that of youthful achievements, such as the *Virgin of the Rocks.* It has supple modelling and the over-elastic attitudes, in which the bony substructure is apt to disappear altogether.

Taking into account the methods dear to Leonardo, among his endless hesitations, it would be over-bold to attempt a solution of so delicate a problem of chronology furnished by documents in the archives. Let us be content, at present, to study the different phases through which the *Adoration of the Magi* passed before taking form in the Uffizi cartoon. We can trace these step by step in a number of drawings.

The earliest of the sketches preserved in the museum on the Rue Bassano, in which Leon Bonnat has collected so many mementos of the great masters, shows that Leonardo's first intention was to paint an *Adoration of the Shepherds,* or *Nativity,* a subject we know him to have painted for the Emperor Maximilian. It represents the infant Jesus lying on the ground with the Virgin adoring and a child bending over Him.

Nude figures are grouped to the right and left, one which seems to have been inspired by the Silenus of the ancients, with his bald head, his long beard and the protuberant belly under his crossed arms,. This strange figure reappears in a drawing formerly in the Armand collection, now in that of Valton.

In short, there is not a figure in the group that does not testify to the enormous amount of work bestowed on the composition.

The spectators on either side call for our special attention. Some are full of majesty while others of eager animation. They are grouped with inimitable ease and liberty. By an artifice, the secrets of which were known to only the greatest dramatists, Leonardo opposes the calm of the people standing at the extremities and framing the composition, so to speak, to the emotional and passionate gestures of those who press towards the Virgin, or kneel before her.

Here, again, Raphael was inspired by Leonardo; he borrowed several of the worshippers placed to the left in his *Dispute of the Sacrament,* one of the most animated and eloquent of his groups. This imitation is very evident in a drawing in the late Duc d'Aumale's collection. Three of the figures – the old man leaning forward, the young man in profile beside him and the man with his back to the spectator in the foreground – are almost exactly reproduced; as is the person standing on the extreme left, wrapped in a cloak with his chin resting on his hand. The breadth and majesty of this last figure inspired yet another artist, more powerful and original than Raphael, an artist who was always ready to cry out against plagiarism, though he himself did not fail to lay the works of his predecessors under contribution. I am referring to Michelangelo. Compare the figure of God the Father in his *Creation of Eve* in the Sistine Chapel with this old man of Leonardo's. The analogy is striking.

In this *Adoration of the Magi,* which biographers have passed over almost in silence, we have, in fact, the germs of two masterpieces by Michelangelo and by Raphael. It is only men of genius like Leonardo who can thus lavish, to some extent unconsciously, treasures which make the fortunes of others, great and small. The background of the cartoon consists of classic ruins with crumbling arches, beneath which are animated groups of men on foot and on horseback; the double staircase is retained and several figures are seated on the steps on one side. Of all the episodes of the sacred story, the Adoration of the Magi is that which lends itself best to the introduction of the gypsy element. It must therefore have been especially attractive to Leonardo, at all times such an ardent lover of horses.

Without transgressing the rules of sacred imagery, he was able to indulge a taste on which, indeed, he had every reason to congratulate himself. He accordingly gives us some dozen horses in every variety of attitudes: lying down, standing, resting, walking, rearing and galloping. In the background to the right we have a regular cavalry skirmish, a forerunner of that in the *Battle of Anghiari*; naked combatants struggling among the feet of horses on the ground, a naked woman flying in terror and so on.

Study for the Madonna and the Child with a Cat, c. 1478-1481. Pen and ink, 13.2 x 9.6 cm. British Museum, London.

One of the most learned of our modern art historians has given an excellent analysis of the technique of the cartoon: "Leonardo," he says, "first made a very careful drawing with pen or brush on the prepared panel; he put the whole into perspective, as the drawing in the Uffizi shows; he then shaded with brown colour; but as he made use of a kind of bitumen, it has lowered very much in tone and, in his finished works, this bituminous colour has absorbed all the others and blackened the shadows extravagantly."

Vasari, too, described Leonardo's innovations in much the same tone: "He introduced a certain darkness into oil painting, which the moderns have adopted to give greater vigour and relief to their figures... Anxious to relieve the objects he represented as much as possible, he strove to produce the most intense blacks by means of dark shadows and thus to make the luminous parts of his pictures more brilliant; the result being that he gradually suppressed the highlights and that his pictures have the effect of night-pieces."

Unconsciously or deliberately, Leonardo shows predilections no less pronounced with regard to colour harmonies. For the more or less crude harmonies of his predecessors, he substituted a subtle scale comprised of subdued tints, such as bistre and bitumen; in these matters he was more ingenious than Rembrandt himself. Here the theorist confirmed the tendencies of the practitioner. We must read chapter XXIV of the *Trattato della Pittura* to see with what irony he rallies the mediocre painters who hide their incompetence under a blaze of gold and ultramarine.

These various analyses will make it easy for us to characterize the progress realized, or I should perhaps say, the revolution accomplished, by Leonardo in painting. Studying nature with passion and all the sciences that tend to its more perfect reproduction – anatomy, perspective, physiognomy – and consulting classic models while preserving all the independence proper to his character, he could not fail to combine precision with liberty and truth with beauty. It is in this final emancipation, this perfect mastery of modelling, illumination and expression, this breadth and freedom, of which the master's *raison d'être* and glory consists. Others may have struck out new paths also; but none travelled further or mounted higher.

The best informed of his biographers, the excellent Vasari, has well defined what was, in some sort, a providential mission. After enumerating all the artistic leaders of the fifteenth century, he adds: "The works of Leonardo da Vinci demonstrated the errors of these artists most completely. He inaugurated the third, or modern manner. Besides the boldness and brilliance of his drawing, the perfection with which he reproduced the most subtle minutiae of nature, he seemed to give actual breath and movement to his figures, thanks to the excellence of his theory, the superiority of his composition, the precision of his proportions, the beauty of his design and his exquisite grace; the wealth of his resources was only equalled by the depth of his art" ("*abbondantissimo di copie, profondissimo di arte*"). It would be difficult to say more happily that the supreme evolution of painting is due to Leonardo.

The first thing that strikes us in considering this period of Leonardo's activity (from 1472, when he was received a member of the Guild of Painters at Florence, to 1482 or 1483, the date of his departure for Milan) is the extreme rarity of his works. Some two or three pictures and sketches are all we can point to as the fruits of these twelve years. And yet, vast cycles were projected and begun at this period in Florence and in Rome. How was it that the patrons of the day neglected the glorious debutant? The reason is not hard to find. By this time Leonardo's tendencies were familiar to all. It was known, on the one hand, that he had little taste for large compositions with numerous figures, such as frescos; and, on the other, that his strivings after an almost superhuman perfection often led to the abandonment of a work he had undertaken.

To a nature so essentially aristocratic as that of Leonardo, the horizon of Florence may well have seemed somewhat limited. The artist was probably ill at ease in a society that was radically middle-class; for popular prejudice against the nobility and all that recalled the bygone tyranny, had lost nothing of its intensity; the Medici of the fifteenth century,

The Adoration of the Magi (study),
1481.
Pen and brown ink,
28.4 x 21.3 cm.
Musée du Louvre, Paris.

Cosimo, Piero and Lorenzo the Magnificent, had constantly to reckon with it, in spite of their omnipotence. Munificent as these wealthy bankers and merchants were, they could not dispense honours, places and treasure like the sovereign princes. In a community in which an irritable spirit of equality still reigned, the artist had perforce to live modestly and plainly. This was bondage for a spirit as brilliant and exuberant as Leonardo! The luxury of a Court, magnificent *fetes* to organize, grandiose experiments to institute, a brilliant destiny to conquer; all these were attractions that were inevitably to draw him, sooner or later, to those elegant, refined and corrupt despots to whom most of the states of Italy were subject at the time.

Plausible as Richter's hypothesis of a trip to the Orient is and strongly possible, as some learned authorities have supported it, I think we must accept it with great reserve. Leonardo, whose imagination was always at work, may have gleaned information about the East from a variety of sources. An indefatigable compiler (some third of his manuscripts consists of extracts from ancient or modern authors), he may have transcribed documents composed by others, without taking the trouble to inform the reader (who was indeed, himself only, for he does not seem to have wished his writings to be printed), that he was not giving his own testimony, but quoting that of others.

In any case, these fragments cannot be accepted as proof of his having travelled in the East, or of his supposed conversion to Islam. Leonardo was passionately fond of geography; geographical allusions, itineraries, descriptions of places, outline maps and topographical sketches occur frequently in his writings. It is not surprising, therefore, that he, a skilled writer, should have projected a sort of romance in the form of letters, the scene of which was to be Asia Minor, a region concerning which contemporary works and perhaps the descriptions of some travelled friend, had supplied him with elements more or less fantastic.

Abandoning this theory of a sojourn in the East, we have still to enquire into the circumstances which led to Leonardo's establishment at the Court of the Sforzi, so famous for its splendor and its corruption. What was the date of this memorable migration, which resulted not only in the creation of the Milanese school, but in setting the seal of perfection on the master's own works? The author of the anonymous life of Leonardo published by Milanesi says that the artist was thirty years old when Lorenzo the Magnificent sent him, with Atalante Miglisrotti, to present a lute to the Duke of Milan. However, according to Vasari, Leonardo took this journey on his own initiative.

In spite of the mystery that rests on the first period of Leonardo's life, we are justified in saying that at an age when other artists are still in search of their true vocation, he had already grappled with the most diverse branches of human learning and that in painting, he had developed a style so individual that posterity has agreed to call it by the name of its inventor. Instruction has but slight influence on natures as profoundly original as his; and on the whole Leonardo, like Michelangelo, would have received little from his master beyond some general indications and the revelation of certain technical processes. If his early career nevertheless lacked the *éclat* that marked Michelangelo's beginnings, it was the result of the fundamental difference of their genius. Leonardo, the dreamer, the enquirer, the experimentalist, pursued an infinity of problems and was as deeply interested in processes as in results.

Thus, Buonarroti had all Florence for his worshippers from the first, whereas Leonardo, appreciated only by a few of the subtler spirits, had to seek his fortune elsewhere. It is not a matter for regret, as far as his own fame is concerned; but it has robbed Florence of one of her titles to glory.

The Adoration of the Magi,
1481-1482.
Yellow ochre and brown ink on
wood panel, 246 x 243 cm.
Galleria degli Uffizi, Florence.

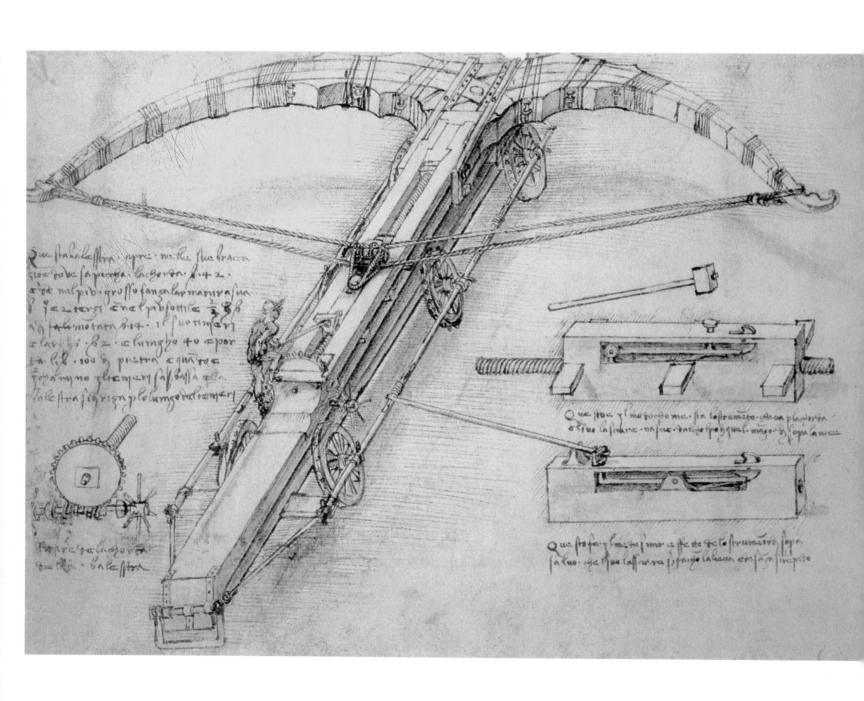

II. THE COURT OF THE SFORZI, THE VIRGIN OF THE ROCKS AND THE MASTERPIECE OF SANTA MARIA DELLE GRAZIE

The Court of the Sforzi

LEONARDO'S sojourn in Milan coincides with Italy's last days of brightness and with the dawn of a martyrdom that was to last three and a half centuries. The year 1490 is the fateful date that marks both the culminating points of a long series of successes and what we should now call the beginning of the end.

Before studying the masterpieces created by Leonardo's genius in Milan and his influence on the Milanese School, to which he gave a new inspiration and direction, just as Raphael did to the Roman School, we must glance at the Court of the Sforzi, his new patrons and inquire what elements this milieu, at once youthful and suggestive, could add to the rich and varied treasure the newcomer brought with him from Florence.

Born at Vigevano on 3 April 1451, the fourth son of Francesco Sforza, Lodovico was early noted for his physical and mental qualities.

Lodovico had the blood of the Visconti in his veins. His mother, as we have said, was the daughter of the last representative of that famous house. From his grandfather, Filippo Maria, he inherited both cowardice and craft; a short sighted craft, however, that finally turned to his own disadvantage. Vacillating and uncertain, a man of schemes rather than of action, he was forever laboriously spinning webs, through which the most blundering of bluebottles could pass with ease.

To epicureans such as the Italians a liberality unaccompanied by the encouragement of letters, of science and art, would have failed altogether in its object. No political propaganda was as effectual as the erection of a sumptuous building, the ordering of a statue or a fresco signed by a famous name. Lodovico, though his statesmanship was narrow and although in a sense he took no thought for the morrow, never neglected this rule. He never relaxed his efforts to attract from far and near, anyone who could add to his glory – writers who would sing his praises, artists who would multiply his portraits.

In dealing with philosophers, poets, historians and men of learning in general, Lodovico – we cannot repeat this too often – hesitates and gropes. In dealing with artists, on the contrary, his judgment is absolutely unerring. Countless documents record with the solicitude and vigilance he used to direct the activity of the army of architects, sculptors, painters, goldsmiths, artists and artificers of every description enrolled by him. He drew up the programme of their creations, superintended their execution, corrected, hastened, scolded them with a vivacity that bears witness both to an ardent love of glory and to a most enlightened taste.

In what light did the Maecenas and the artist see each other? How did these two emancipated spirits react to one another and what effect did their reciprocal involvement exercise upon art, science, philosophy, and the many lofty qualities embodied in Leonardo? Their minds were not without striking analogies. At once subtle and vacillating, Lodovico did his utmost to impose his own idiosyncrasy on his interpreters. Let us hear what Paolo Giovio, the priestly chronicler, said of him: "Lodovico had caused Italy to be represented in a hall of his palace as a queen, accompanied by a Moorish squire (in allusion to his complexion or his device), bearing a musket. He sought to show by this allegory that he was arbiter of the national destinies and that it was his mission to defend his country against all attack."

When, in 1483, Leonardo came to seek his fortune at Lodovico's court, the prince had been governing Milan for four years. His subjects had therefore had time to gain some idea of his character and tastes. Leonardo, who was sure to have gathered such information concerning his new master, seemed to have been quite aware of the duke's weakness for the

The Giant Crossbow, 1480-1482.
Pen and ink.
Pinacoteca Ambrosiana, Milan.

occult sciences. This, at any rate, was the string he played upon in Lodovico by the aid of a programme bewildering in its variety.

He proceeded to celebrate the virtues of his new patron in a series of allegories in which he represented him wearing spectacles and standing between Envy and Justice, the latter painted black (an allusion to il Moro's dark complexion again); now as Fortune or as victory over Poverty, covering with a corner of his ducal mantle a youth pursued by the hideous hag and protecting him with a wand.

Despite the many affinities between the artist and his patron, there is nothing to prove that Leonardo was among il Moro's intimates.

It is not without a certain approval that we recognize an indifferent courtier in the great artist and thinker. Though he had to reproach himself with many weaknesses, Leonardo never owed success to an astutely woven intrigue.

It would be hopeless to attempt to disentangle any exact conclusions as to Leonardo's financial situation while in Lodovico's services from the complicated public accounts of the period. Besides a fixed salary, he probably received sums in proportion to the importance of his work (according to Bandello, he had 2,000 ducats per annum during the execution of the *Last Supper*).

Leonardo's own ideas as to the respective value of the different arts were summed up, according to Lomazzo, in this maxim: the more an art involves physical fatigue, the better it is.

It has often been maintained that the change in Leonardo's style in his new place of residence was due to the influence of the school he found there. "A Florentine when he arrived in Milan," writes Marchesa d'Adda, "Leonardo left it a Milanese."

Further on he adds: "An art, peculiar to and savouring of its native soil, sprang up in Lombardy from the union of Tuscan and Paduan traditions. Mantegna had Milanese disciples who took with them the traditions of Squarcione. The works of the elder Foppa, Leonardo da Besozzo, Buttinone, Civerchio, Troso da Monza and Zenale da Treviglio, are proof enough that a veritable and even highly-developed art existed in Milan long before the arrival of Leonardo."

Was the change in Leonardo as distinctly marked as they would have us believe and moreover, did the example of the Lombard artists count for so much in it as is asserted? I do not hesitate to answer no and for these reasons: the works executed at the beginning of his sojourn in Milan, the *Virgin of the Rocks,* was proof that the youthful Leonardo was already gifted with elegance, sweetness and grace in a greater degree than any master who had preceded him. On the other hand, no genius was more rebellious to the teachings and suggestions of others.

After all, what were these Lombard masters whom we are to look upon as the teachers of the Florentine Proteus? Leonardo's manner, on the contrary, rests on the suppression of all that is angular and precise; his painting is above all things fused, melting, enveloped; the outlines of his figures lose themselves in the intensity of light and in the harmony of colour. Again, the Milanese primitives assiduously cultivated the fresco, whereas Leonardo, unfortunately, persistently avoided that process during his stay in Milan and also after his return to Florence. He painted the *Last Supper* in oil and prepared to paint the *Battle of Anghiari* in encaustic.

As for Leonardo, it was by considerable resources; the brilliant festivals, the intercourse with intellectual and distinguished men and, above all, the less *bourgeois* and democratic atmosphere than that of Florence, that the sudden and unprecedented evolution of his genius was brought about. In Florence he would have become the best of painters; at Milan, he became that as well as a great poet and a great thinker. From this point of view we have every right to say that he owed much to his new country.

If, with the exception of Bramante, Milan possessed no other artist capable of measuring himself with Leonardo, or any capable of influencing him, then no other surroundings could have been more propitious to his genius than those it offered. A pleasure-seeking and enlightened prince and an active, wealthy and educated population, a phalanx of capable artists who asked for nothing better than to follow the lead of a mastermind from Florence whence the light has been shed for so long over Italy; finally, the vigorous and inspiring

Profile of Warrior as tournament captain, c.1480.
Silver point on prepared ivory,
28.5 x 21 cm.
British Museum, London.

Study for the Fight Against the Dragon, c. 1480.
Pen and ink, grey wash,
19 x 12.5 cm.
Musée du Louvre, Paris. (p. 34, 35)

Léonard de Vinci.

suggestions of a landscape at once exuberant and grandiose; can we imagine elements better suited than these to stimulate the genius of Leonardo and to kindle in his love for the country he was now to make his own?

When Leonardo resolved himself to try his luck at the court of the Sforzi he was already known there by the famous shield acquired by Duke Galeazzo Maria (died in 1476).

We possess a remarkable document in the Leonardo's own hand that bears upon his opening relations with the Milanese capital, namely, the letter in which he offers his services to Lodovico il Moro, the regent of the duchy for his nephew Gian Galeazzo. This epistle can hardly be called a monument of diffidence, as the reader will presently have an opportunity to judge; in it the painter, the sculptor, the architect, the military and hydraulic engineer, come forward and make their boast in turn:

"Having, most illustrious lord, seen and duly considered the experiments of all those who repute themselves masters in the art of inventing instruments of war and having found that their instruments differ in no way from such as are in common use, I will endeavour, without wishing to injure any one else, to make known to your Excellency certain secrets of my own; as briefly enumerated here below:

"1. I have a way of constructing very light bridges, most easy to carry, by which the enemy may be pursued and put to flight, and others also of a stronger kind, which resists fire or assault, and are easy to place and remove. I know ways also for burning and destroying those of the enemy.

"2. In case of laying siege to a place I know how to remove the water from ditches and to make various scaling ladders and other such instruments.

"3. Item: If, on account of the height or strength of position, the place cannot be bombarded, I have a way for ruining every fortress which is not on stone foundations.

"4. I can also make a kind of cannon, easy and convenient to transport, that will discharge inflammable matters, causing great injury to the enemy and also great terror from the smoke.

"5. Item: By means of winding and narrow underground passages, made without noise, I can contrive a way for passing under ditches or any stream.

"6. (sic) And, if the fight should be at sea, I have numerous engines of the utmost activity both for attack and defence; vessels that will resist the heaviest fire – also powders or vapours.

"7. Item: I can construct covered carts, secure and indestructible, bearing artillery, which, upon entering among the enemy, will break the strongest body of men and which the infantry can follow without impediment.

"8. I can construct cannon, mortars and fire-engines of beautiful and useful shape and different from those in common use.

"9. Where the use of cannon is impracticable, I can replace them by catapults, mangonels and engines for discharging missiles of admirable efficacy and hitherto unknown – in short, I can contrive endless means of offence.

"10. In times of peace, I believe I can equal any one in architecture and in constructing buildings, public or private and in conducting water from one place to another.

"Then I can execute sculpture, whether in marble, bronze, or terracotta; also in painting I can do as much as any other, be he who he may.

"Furthermore, I can execute a bronze horse in lasting memory of your father and of the illustrious house of Sforza and, if any of the above-mentioned things should appear impossible and impracticable to you, I offer to make trial of them in your park, or in any other place that may please your Excellency, to whom I commend myself in utmost humility."

In all probability, Leonardo set to work immediately after his arrival in Milan upon the equestrian statue of Francesco Sforza, an undertaking that occupied him, at intervals, for seventeen years.

Rumours of discussions that had been going on for ten years concerning the choice of a suitable design must, of course, have reached Leonardo and in the memorial addressed to Lodovico, he declares himself ready – as we have seen – to undertake the execution of the "cavallo", the name given to the equestrian statue.

Allegorical Representations of Various Figures of Women,
c. 1480.
Pen and ink on stylet,
22.5 x 20.2 cm.
Brtitish Museum, London.

Had Leonardo remained in Florence, he may very easily have painted a *Last Supper* equal to that of Santa Maria delle Grazie for a monastery in his native city, but he most certainly would never have been commissioned to execute a piece of sculpture such as the equestrian statue of Duke Francesco, as conspicuous in dimensions as the idea of supremacy, it was calculated to impress the beholder.

The doctrine of equality, so jealously insisted upon by the Florentine populace, had long relegated sculpture to the sphere of religion; the utmost that the Republic had done in any other spirit being to accord the honour of monumental tombs to its chancellors, Leonardo Bruni and Carlo Marsuppini. To have set up in a public place the statue of a condottiere and, worse still, one whose family still claimed sovereignty would have raised a storm of indignation among the keenly susceptible citizens. As well as propose that they should return to the worship of graven images! Hence any Florentine sculptor who wished to execute monumental statues was forced to seek such commissions elsewhere than at home, as did Donatello in Padua (the equestrian statue of Gattamelata); Baroncelli in Ferrara (the equestrian statue of Niccolò d'Este), Verrocchio in Venice (the equestrian statue of Colleone) and, lastly, Leonardo in Milan.

Leonardo was not one to make rapid decisions and Lodovico il Moro did not possess the fortitude to make a plan and strictly keep to it; no doubt, his much-admired artist unsettled his mind anew each time they met by laying a new design before him.

As we have already seen, he made suggestions after suggestions – now the huge pedestal was circular, now rectangular, now in the shape of a rotunda, now a triumphal arch; then again, it was to surmount a deep cavity containing the recumbent figure of the deceased Duke and so forth.

Finally, Sforza, worn out by these incessant discussions, begged Pietro Alemanni, the Florentine ambassador at Milan, to ask Lorenzo the Magnificent to send him one or two sculptors capable of executing the statue in question. The Duke, adds Alemanni, being afraid that Leonardo - who had been commissioned to make the model - was hardly equal to the task!

This threat to supplant him evidently had the desired effect of rousing Leonardo from his apathy, now we have indubitable proof that by the following year the work was once more in full swing. On the date of 23 April, we find this entry among his memoranda: "Today I began this book and recommenced the 'horse' (the equestrian statue)."

At last on 30 November 1493, the date of the marriage of Bianca Maria Sforza to the Emperor Maximilian, the model of the horse was exhibited to the public under a triumphal arch.

This was the end of the first act of the drama; the second opened with the necessary preparations for the casting of the statue. Strictly speaking, the sculptor may now have considered his part of the business completed because the remaining work was chiefly mechanical.

But the division of labour was not clearly defined in the fifteenth century and Leonardo was obliged to devote a lot of time and patience to experiments in the founder's art. The construction of the furnaces and the moulds, the composition of the bronze, the manner of heating, the finishing of the cast, the polishing, the chasing – all this had to be carefully considered.

Leonardo's masterpiece came to a miserable end. Sabba di Castiglione's story of the statue being knocked to pieces by the Gascon crossbowmen of Louis XII was perhaps taken too literally.

Study for The Trivulzio Equestrian Monument, 1508-1511. Pen and bistre, 28 x 19.8 cm. Royal Library, Windsor Castle.

The proof that this ruthless destruction did not occur during Louis's first occupation of Milan in 1499 is evident from the fact that in 1501 the Duke of Ferrara was anxious to obtain possession of the model executed by Leonardo.

Still, we have no reason to doubt that foreign soldiers had a hand in this deplorable piece of vandalism, though there is probably much justice in Bonnaffé's presumption that: "A statue of perishable material, of such dimensions and in such an attitude, exposed to all the vicissitudes of the weather soon perishes when it once begins to deteriorate."

Already very damaged in 1501, Leonardo's monument was inevitably doomed.

All the information we have concerning the other sculptures by Leonardo is more or less open to question. Among the works ascribed to him are: *The Infant Jesus Blessing the Little St John*, a terracotta, formerly the property of Cardinal Federigo Borromeo and a *St Jerome*, a high relief, formerly in the Hugford collection at Florence.

According to Rio, Leonardo even worked using ivory! This uncritical writer remarks that "Thiers owns a little ivory figure of exquisite workmanship, which can hardly be attributed to any one but Leonardo". It is enough to reproduce such an assertion to show its inanity!

Needless to say, the sculpture of the School of Milan fell under Leonardo's ascendancy no less evidently than the painting. Indeed, the principles of the creator of the equestrian statue of Francesco Sforza and of the *Last Supper* were so suggestive that they extended their influence even into regions apparently inaccessible to their action. It appears in unexpected artists like Bernardino Luini and Sodom, who never had the good fortune to come into personal contact with Leonardo. This influence, however, did not manifest itself everywhere with identical or equally beneficial results. Though the Milanese sculptors recognized the supreme grace of Leonardo's creation and, to a certain extent, the difficulties that he had overcome, they had no conception of the infinite amount of detailed research and strenuous labour that went into making up the sum of his perfection. Hence it was that Milanese sculpture passed from extreme ruggedness to the facility, the polish, and the sentimental insipidity so apparent in the statues and bas-reliefs of Briosco at the Certosa of Pavia and those of Bambaja, on the famous tomb of Gaston de Foix.

The Virgin of the Rocks

In the history of modern art there is no bigger problem than the classification and the chronology of Leonardo da Vinci's works. It is sometimes tempting to believe that just as the master's handwriting remained absolutely unchanged for thirty-five years making it impossible to distinguish the manuscripts of his extreme old age from those of his first literary

Study for The Sforza Equestrian Monument, c. 1485-1490. Metalpoint on blue prepared paper, 11.6 x 10.3 cm. Royal Library, Windsor Castle.

efforts. His manner of drawing and painting never varied an iota throughout his career. In these types of investigations it is impossible to show too much reserve, scepticism and above all modesty, a virtue that is becoming extremely rare in the domain of artistic erudition. But I may offer some materials for the building up of a monument that no isolated efforts can hope to raise. Successive biographers of Leonardo have fixed the date of the *Virgin of the Rocks*— some before his removal from Florence, some after his establishment at Milan—in other words, some before and after the year 1484. A document has answered this vexed question; the picture was painted at Milan.

Nevertheless, there is a vast gulf between the Louvre picture and other works painted by Leonardo in Milan; the technique, style and expression all differ. The drawing is slightly dry and hard, somewhat in the manner of Verrocchio; the crumpled draperies, the anxious, even fretful expression of the faces are peculiarities (we dare not say faults, for such faults disarm criticism) that disappeared in the master's more mature works. In a word, though it was painted in Milan, the *Virgin of the Rocks* is Florentine in feeling.

The painting, in spite of the impression of rapid and spontaneous creation it gives the spectator was one of the most laborious of the master's works, as his drawings bear witness. A characteristic drawing in the École des Beaux Arts reveals the various transformations of a single figure, notably that of the angel.

He appears first in profile, standing, his left foot on a step, with one hand he holds his mantle and with the other he points to some object unseen in the drawing, evidently to the little St John. On the lower section are studies in silver-point for the left arm that is holding back the drapery and for the right arm which appears first with the hand extended, then with the hand closed, save for the first finger. This last is the action Leonardo finally adopted for the picture.

I hasten to add that it is also the only part of the drawing he kept. In the picture the angel is no longer in profile, but turns his face three-quarters to the spectator which adds greatly to the animation of the scene because in a composition of four people, two of whom are children, an actor in profile would be more or less lost. The action of the left arm has undergone a very important modification; instead of holding the drapery, it supports the Divine Child and the angel, who was standing, now kneels on one knee. It needed Leonardo's consummate art to mask so much effort and to preserve an appearance of freshness and spontaneity in a work that was the result of long and elaborate combinations.

A decisive argument in favour of the authenticity of the Louvre picture is furnished by the fact that there are studies by Leonardo in the École des Beaux Arts and at Windsor showing the angel's hand stretched towards the Infant Jesus. As is well known, this gesture is modified in the London example which must therefore come from a later date.

In the first of these drawings, which has escaped the investigations of all my predecessors, the standing figure certainly seems to have been re-touched and perhaps even re-drawn in parts, but the two fragments of the arms and hands proclaim Leonardo's authorship with unmistakable precision. Note that the angel's arm resembles that of St Peter in the *Last Supper* in Milan - there is the same gesture, the same bending back of the hand.

The London picture is, in my opinion, a replica, painted under Leonardo's supervision by one of his pupils. The Louvre picture has a hard aspect and harsh tonality. Time has fastened his cruel teeth into it. The painting has lost its bloom and the groundwork seems to lie bare before us. Nevertheless, it speaks to the eyes and the soul with supreme authority.

We must further remember that the Louvre picture has a venerable history. It has been on the spot for hundreds of years. In the first part of the sixteenth century it was already in the collection of Francis I, a sovereign, who was very favourably circumstanced in regards to the acquisition of works by Leonardo.

The differences between the London and Paris examples are of precisely the same nature as those of the two examples of Holbein's *Madonna*, in the Dresden Gallery and the example in the Darmstadt Museum. The first, the original, is more archaic and heavy but more deeply felt; the second, the copy, is freer and more elegant.

Virgin of the Rocks (detail),
1491-1508.
Oil on canvas, 189.5 x 120 cm.
The National Gallery, London.

Virgin of the Rocks, 1483-1486.
Oil on canvas, 199 x 122 cm.
Musée du Louvre, Paris.

Virgin of the Rocks, 1491-1508.
Oil on wood panel,
189.5 x 120 cm.
The National Gallery, London.

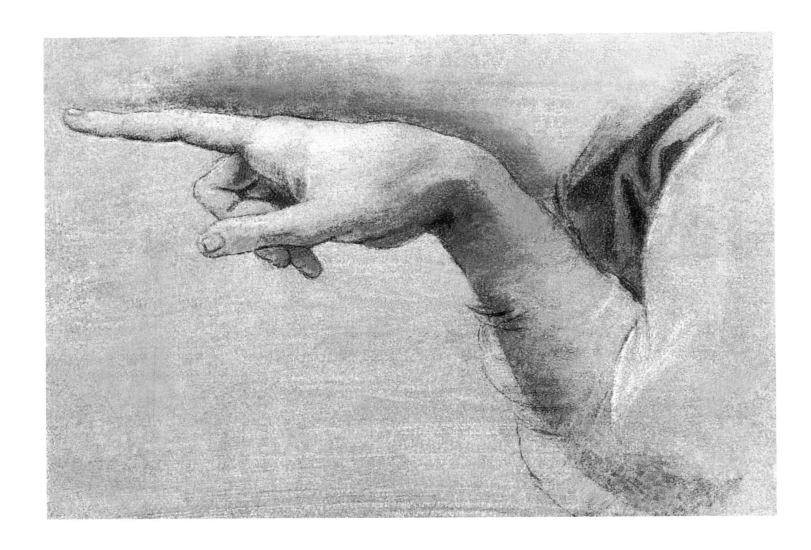

If the National Gallery picture was painted in Leonardo's studio and under his supervision, it is easy to see why certain harshness is apparent in the Louvre example has disappeared in that of the National Gallery. The master was seeking, hesitating; the pupil had only to copy and to soften.

It is time to study the composition of the *Virgin of the Rocks*.

It is a group of four figures, three kneeling, the fourth seated at the entrance of a cavern. These figures are arranged in the pyramidal, a form very much appreciated by Raphael. The Virgin is at the centre and in the middle ground the other actors dominate. A blue mantle, fastened at the breast by a brooch hangs from her shoulders. One hand on the shoulder of the infant St John, at whom she is looking, the other extended over her Son while she invites the precursor to approach him. The Infant is seated on the ground and steadying himself with his left hand and blesses his young companion with the right hand. The angel places one knee on the ground beside the Child and supports him with one hand and with the other hand shows him the infant St John. Here we already have the germs of the consummate art of gesture, which Leonardo made so brilliant after the application in the *Last Supper* in Milan. It is this aspect that gives such extraordinary animation to the composition.

The master, however, is still far from perfect. Certain inexperience is revealed along with the most exquisite sensibility and the rarest faculty of observation. There is, in particular, something slightly archaic in the Virgin's style. (The painter seems to have lagged behind the draftsman because the studies for this picture are free and supple in the highest degree.) The nose is straight, not aquiline, the mouth is slightly curved, the chin low and square, as in certain faces of Perugino's and Francia's. As for the angel who wears a red tunic and a green mantle, his expression is vague and undecided. He is more firmly modelled in the two preliminary drawings, the one in the Royal Library in Turin, the other at the École des Beaux Arts. Note the affinity between his type and that of the Virgin.

Study of a Hand, c. 1483.
Black chalk with white
highlights, 15.3 x 22 cm.
Royal Library, Windsor Castle.

44

The two children also possess something hard and arid; the desire for objective truth occasionally overcomes a sense of style and expression. But what a knowledge of color and modelling! The result is a mixture of Correggio and Rembrandt. In the Infant Jesus, with his somewhat mournful expression, his chestnut locks, his chubby contours (there are dimples on the elbow and shoulder), the effect of the wonderful foreshortening and the broadly treated surfaces is short of miraculous. In the infant St John, the foreshortening is curt and abrupt much like the manner of Verrocchio. The type, too, has striking analogies with those of Verrocchio. I may add that the light falls full on the Infant Saviour, whereas his young companion is in shadow.

It is not easy to sum up the beauties of such a work. First of all, I must point out the profound originality of the conception and the infinite charm of the execution. Like a balloon soaring in the air to such a height that presently all but a few points on the earth are out of sight, it rises above all anterior and contemporary works! Once more an artist has arisen, who, casting off the trammels of tradition looks at things face to face and renders them as he sees them with sovereign grace and distinction. Before Raphael, Leonardo treats the little intimate drama: the Virgin caressing her son, watching his play, directing his education – and treats it with as much charm, if not with quite the same precision of touch. The playfulness, the lightness and, at the same time the conviction with which he endows these scenes of two or three actors can not be rendered in words. They are ideals of the freshest and most innocent kind, without that note of melancholy or that prescience of pain to come that often puts in the eyes and on the lips of the young mother.

The composition is curiously modern. There is a large amount of freedom, even in the faces! The artist, unfettered by traditional portraits takes as model for the Virgin, Christ, the Apostles and Saints, the men and women around him. He troubles himself little about attributes preserving or suppressing them according to the exigencies of his scheme. He goes so far as to represent the Virgin with bare feet; heresy into which Fra Angelico, nourished in the severe tradition of the Dominicans would never have fallen, a heresy which orthodox painters abjured once more after the Council of Trent.

But if Leonardo, like the majority of his Florentine contemporaries, brought his divinities down to earth then he gave warmth and poetry to his conceptions which were well calculated to awaken religious fervor and there is no other painter that has passed for a more devout artist. Leonardo and Perugino, the two artists Vasari charges with absolute scepticism, are the two whose works breathe most eloquently of faith!

Leaving warmth and intensity of harmony to his fellow-student, Perugino, with his deep and brilliant greens and reds, his precise contours, his firm and often hard modelling, Leonardo, in his *Virgin of the Rocks,* as in all his later works, determined to win colour from very neutral shades, greens verging on greys, with silvery reflections, bitumen, and dull yellow.

Nothing was so strongly opposed to the scale adopted by the primitives. All high and blunt tones were banished from his palette such as gold, other rich colours and brilliant carnations. It was indeed, with sort a of *Camaïeu* that he achieved his marvels of chiaroscuro and the incomparable warmth and amber harmony of his *Mona Lisa.* No artist before him had made so severe a demand on the possibilities of pure painting.

The ease of the composition and the richness of the handling claim our admiration in equal degree. The Florentines may have justly exclaimed: "At last a painter is born to us!" The angles and articulations of the figures have disappeared giving way to harmonious lines. These in turn are bathed in light of infinite suavity or, rather, the figures themselves are conceived with a view of the light that bathes them. This art of wrapping objects in the atmosphere was, in fact, if not invented by Leonardo, at least first brought by him to a high degree of perfection which it now attains.

In his effects of chiaroscuro, in the unprecedented subtleties of his colour harmonies, we recognize the born painter.

Leonardo was as well versed in the laws of linear perspective, anatomy and kindred sciences as any of his rivals. Far from looking upon them as an end in themselves he treated them as accessories, a mechanism, to be concealed as soon as they have played their part. A picture, according to his idea, should betray no effort meaning it must only show the result – the ideal of grace, beauty, or harmony in full perfection.

The landscape of the *Virgin of the Rocks* calls for special analysis.

From the beginning, Leonardo preferred rocky and broken landscapes over scenes with broad lines and undulations. The Italian painting of the Renaissance hovered between these two tendencies. One was followed by the "trecentisti", whose successor Leonardo was at this point, the other by Perugino and to some extent, by the Venetians. The partisans of the first system affected marked contrasts such as rugged boulders alternating with smiling vegetation or scenery tunneled by ravines and ravaged by convulsions, as in some parts of the Apennines. They are one with the Flemings in their love of detail. The others lean towards large surfaces while their hills descend into plains and lakes by gradual undulations. Their landscapes are representations of the Roman Campagna rendered with masterly effect by Perugino and the Umbrian school.

Leonardo, however, loved to complicate and refine upon traditional materials. The gorges of Chiusuri and of Monte Oliveto were not sufficient. He was not even content with the erratic boulders of the monastery of La Vernia, in the Casentino. The mineralogist and geologist dominated the artist. He was fascinated by the strange and monstrous dolomite rocks of the Friuli and its gigantic cones emerging from vast tablelands, jagged peaks, grottos no less imposing than the dolmens and menhirs of Brittany.

The soil was treated with all the tenderness that the Primitives bestowed on accessories. Mantegna could not have been more exact, but Leonardo adds fancy to exactitude. Slabs of rocks, pebbles, plants (irises), make up the foreground.

The grotto seemed to breathe forth a strange and penetrating moisture: we dream of nymphs, sylphs, gnomes and of all the fantasy world evoked by Shakespeare in *A Midsummer Night's Dream,* a world only Leonardo could have translated on canvas. The background is composed of a series of perpendicular rocks that look like sugar loaves.

Leonardo, even though his spirit was hesitant, shows a rare tenacity in his choice of landscape motifs. Throughout his works, in the *Virgin of the Rocks,* the *St Anne* and the *Mona Lisa,* we find the same dolomite mountains with abrupt peaks rising from high plains in bizarre outline. He probably made a journey in his youth through the Friuli and retained a vivid recollection of its scenery.

It is most likely impossible that the famous *Madonna Litta,* bought in Milan for the Hermitage in Saint Petersburg in 1865 may also have been painted during this period.

The fact that the beautiful profile study for the Virgin's head in the Vallardi collection at the Louvre is on the same greenish paper as the studies of the *Virgin of the Rocks* tends to prove that the *Madonna Litta* is a more or less contemporary work. This drawing contains the master's first idea.

In the picture, we see the Virgin seated as a half-length figure in a room with two open windows on an arid landscape. Dressed in a red robe bordered with gold embroidery and a blue mantle lined with yellow, she also wears a greyish scarf striped with black and enriched with gold ornaments on her head, not unlike those worn by Raphael's *Aldobrandini Madonna* and his *Madonna della Sedia.* She gazes tenderly at the Babe offering him her right breast. The Child looks towards the spectator and lays one hand on his mother's breast and grasps a goldfinch in the other. The conception is singularly sincere and touching.

Criticism has wavered considerably in its ascriptions of the *Madonna Litta.* It has been accepted, generally, as a copy of an original by Leonardo. Clement de Ris compared it to Luini, whereas Morelli claimed it for the inevitable Bernardino dei Conti and Harck for the no less inevitable Ambrogio de Predis.

The Masterpiece of Santa Maria delle Grazie

From this point on I propose to show how the painter of the *Mona Lisa,* the *Virgin of the Rocks* and the *Saint Anne* developed, by which teachings of his predecessors he profited, through what intimate vicissitudes his ideas passed before culminating in the immortal page of Santa Maria delle Grazie. In this piece there is no abstract or artificial work born of the artist's imagination, but a page from the book of life itself—a story that has been seen and felt, a drama that has been acted. I have devoted myself to the process, congratulating myself on

The Madonna Litta, c. 1490.
Tempera on canvas, transferred
from a wood panel, 42 x 33 cm.
The State Hermitage Museum,
St. Petersburg.

the fact that my predecessors have confined themselves to the collection of materials and that I have the pleasure of offering my readers an attempt at a coordination of these materials, which, whatever its merit, will at least be novel.

Before entering on this analysis I would like to say a few words pertaining to the origin of the Santa Maria delle Grazie and its destination.

The word "Cenacolo" has a wide usage in Italian. It is used indifferently for a dining-hall or refectory, for the special "upper room" where the Savior ate the Last Supper with his disciples and for a picture representing that holy scene. The church of Santa Maria delle Grazie, the Lombardian architectural masterpiece, was founded by the Dominicans who began its construction in 1464 in the Gothic style.

The history of *The Last Supper* in Santa Maria delle Grazie is buried in obscurity. We do not know when the masterpiece was begun, when it was finished, or the conditions concerning its creation though it is known that Leonardo was at work upon it in 1497 and that he finished it in that year.

Leonardo disliked working in the fresco style because of its demanding process that did not coincide with the speed of his normal working habits. He decided to use oil paint which, in addition to its other qualities, was a new product.

In his religious compositions, Leonardo rarely strayed from the theme of his work. The *Virgin of the Rocks,* the *Adoration of the Magi* and the *John the Baptist* astonish and charm us beyond measure, but they do not possess the same illumination or sophistication.

In his *Last Supper,* the master attacked this problem from the front, bluntly and without subterfuge, determined to stay strictly within the Evangelist's story and to study the subject completely and without bias. Hence because of this strict procedure that the painting in the Santa Maria delle Grazie may be classed with Raphael's cartoons, as a work giving forth the purest evangelic information. It is a work which now believers of every creed come love and a painting that even has the power to rekindle faith.

No picture was ever lingered over more lovingly. It ripened in the artist's mind long before his hand began to translate the image that was engraved on his brain onto canvas. Leonardo thought of it day and night.

We know, however, that Lodovico at last put some pressure on the overly meticulous artist to finish his work. On 30 June 1497, he ordered one of his agents 'to beg' Leonardo to complete his work in the refectory of Santa Maria delle Grazie.

Another sixteenth-century writer, the Milanese Lomazzo, completed Vasari's story explaining why Leonardo left the principal figure unfinished. After endowing the saint, James the Just with the beauty we still admire, across the ruins of *Cenacolo*, Leonardo, desperately trying to convey the face of Christ according to how he dreamt took advice from his old friend Zenale who made this memorably responded: "Leonardo, the fault thou hast committed is one of which God only can absolve thee. In fact, it is impossible to represent a figure more beautiful or soft than James the Just. Accept thy misfortune with patience and leave your imperfect Christ as he is, because, when compared with the apostles, he would not be their Saviour or their Master." Leonardo took his advice and this is why the head of Christ was left a mere sketch.

When comparing this project with the painting, we see that when it was first conceived, the *Last Supper* contained a large number of realistic traits given that the subject was formal. Thus, he deleted the gesture where one of the apostles puts down the glass from which he had begun to drink and the gesture of the apostle holding a loaf he had cut in two. Of the two knives spoken of in the note only one appears in the painting in the hand of St Peter. There is also no apostle shading his eyes with his hand. In short, the action, though less lively and dramatic becomes more imposing and gains in elevation.

A drawing in the Windsor Library where a disciple shades his eyes with his hand is also amongst these pictorial studies. It further contains St John with his head on the tablecloth and another apostle who approaches Jesus with a reverent inclination of the body.

Leonardo, we must conclude, had for a time some thought of representing the institution of the Eucharist, a theme often treated by the Byzantines and one that Justus of Ghent had illustrated a year or two before in a picture he painted for the Duke of Urbino.

The Last Supper (detail),
1495-1498. Oil and tempera on
stone, 460 x 880 cm.
Santa Maria delle Grazie, Milan.

A sketch on the same sheet, where the intention is difficult to determine, shows a group of ten people at table and Judas placed alone on the opposite side as if he were already excluded from interaction with the other disciples. A little later Leonardo broke away from tradition on this point. Instead of following the example of his predecessors and isolating Judas on one side of the table, like a diseased sheep, he conceived the more dramatic idea of placing him side by side with his victim; from this proximity evolved a motive of the most poignant mimetic expression: the explosion of surprise and indignation among the disciples at the Master's revelation of the treachery among them.

We can sum up by saying that the primitive conception of the scene was more or less violent; the master gradually tempered and disciplined his action and it is the expression of condensed and latent power in his final rendering to which he owes his most brilliant triumph.

The perfection of the achieved grouping in the *Last Supper* would in itself be sufficient to mark an epoch in the annals of painting. Its ease and rhythm are indescribable. The figures, placed on two planes in perspective are further arranged in groups of three with the exception of Christ, who, isolated in the centre, dominates the action. Eight of the apostles are represented in profile, three three-quarters to the front; Jesus and St John face the spectator.

The skill and knowledge necessary to bring these trios of heads into relation one with another, to animate the groups without destroying their balance, to vary the lines without detracting from their harmony and finally to connect the various groups were so tremendous that neither reasoning nor calculation could have solved a problem so intricate, but for a sort of divine inspiration the most gifted artist would have failed. I may add that the most perfect sense of line and mass would have proved insufficient without an equally perfect knowledge of chiaroscuro and of aerial perspective, for some of the juxtapositions – for example, the head facing three quarters to the front, relieved against a head in profile – are too daring to have been successfully attempted by means of mere draughtsmanship or linear perspective.

Study for The Last Supper,
c. 1495. Pen and ink.
Galleria dell'Accademia, Venice.

Study for the Head of St James and Architectural Sketches,
c. 1495. Red chalk, pen and ink,
25 x 17 cm.
Royal Library, Windsor Castle.

Finally a new path was opened; Raphael was not slow to follow in the footsteps of Leonardo the pioneer who proved to be a worthy rival, first with his *Dispute of the Sacrament* and afterwards in his *School of Athens.*

The dominant characteristics in these faces are virility, breadth, gravity, and conviction. They indicate free and upright natures and men who have a perfect consciousness of their feelings and are ready to accept the responsibility for their actions. Energy and loyalty are present in every feature. The master has given a great variety of types. (I am speaking less of physical differences, such as the crisp, waving, or curly hair of the various heads, than of moral divergences.)

For example, some figures are plain fishermen transformed into missionaries and he has preserved the proper rudeness to their former calling. Of this class is the apostle to the left of Jesus, who extends his arms and opens his mouth to express his stupefaction. To others – as, for instance, the old man with a long beard on the left, he has given a patriarchal majesty; to others again – such as the beloved disciple and St Philip – the sweetness of the "quattrocento" adolescent, with the resignation of the Christian convert. Judas, with his hooked nose, his bold forehead, his admirably defined silhouette, is a perfect type of the malefactor. It would be impossible to imagine anything more dramatic than these contrasts.

How little affinity there was between such a conception and the delicate refinements and elegances of il Moro's Court! What power and vigour breathe from these actors in a drama which, overflowing the boundaries of its narrow Milanese environment, has thrilled humanity. For four centuries!

If we turn to expression and gesture, we must again make homage to the master's extraordinary perception of dramatic effect. The Saviour has just uttered the fateful words: "One of you shall betray me" with sublime resignation. In a moment, as by an electric shock, he has excited the most diverse emotions among the disciples, according to the character of each. Doubt, surprise, distrust and indignation are manifested by ineffable traits. Souls vibrated in unison from one end of the table to the other. But it was necessary to mingle

The Last Supper, 1495-1498.
Oil and tempera on gesso,
pitch and mastic, 460 x 880 cm.
Santa Maria delle Grazie, Milan.

lighter notes in this epic concert in order to emphasize this outburst of generous feeling. Judas, leaning comfortably on his elbow, the money bag in his right hand, his left opening as if involuntarily when he hears his treachery unmasked, is the personification of the hardened villain, who has justified his crime in his own mind and is bent on carrying it through to the end. St John, his head bowed, his clasped hands on the table, is a perfect type of supreme devotion, gentleness and faith.

Since the time of Giotto, the great dramatist, there has not been an equal attempt to translate the passions of the soul by means of gesture had been made. Leonardo does not make us hear the cries of mothers, whose infants have been torn from them by Herod's executioners, or of the damned, tormented by demons in Hell. His subject demanded treatment less violent than these. But with what consummate art he renders all the intricacies of feeling!

How full of delicate gradation and reticence is his pantomime, entirely free though artificial! How fully we feel the artist's mastery of his subject, nay, more, his perfect participation in the sentiments with which he endows his characters! The *Last Supper* is more than a miracle of art it is Leonardo's heart as well as his imagination and his intellect.

While affirming the principles of idealism throughout the whole of his work, Leonardo has nevertheless endeavoured to give his composition a realistic appearance. Fearing to fall into abstraction he multiplied the details that give a life like illusion. With meticulous care he painted all the accessories to the frugal banquet! The table is laid with dishes, bowls, bottles, glasses that give an opportunity for the play of varied light, rolls of bread, fruit – pears and apples, some with a leaf still clinging to the stalk.

Making a concession to the conventions of his day he did not forget the saltcellar overturned by Judas. He treated the tablecloth itself with the utmost care, marking the folds of the damask, the pattern at the ends and the four-knotted corners. An extremely fastidious observer, which a modern master of style would despise and which Leonardo had learnt from the Primitives, that the picture owes its convincing quality.

St Jerome, 1482. Tempera and oil on wood panel, 103 x 75 cm. Pinacoteca Vaticana, Rome.

Study of an Apostle, c. 1495. Pen over metalpoint on blue background, 14.5 x 11.3 cm. Albertina Museum, Vienna.

Perhaps no other artist, with the exception of Brunellesco, Piero della Francesca and Mantegna had worked out the laws of linear perspective with equal ardour. It would, therefore, have been easy for him to bring the various planes of his compositions into relief by the introduction of buildings. The only works in which we find him making use of this artifice are the *Last Supper* and the cartoon for the *Adoration of the Magi*. Leonardo, however, seemed to have had too deep a veneration for the human form to subordinate it to the exigencies of any architect, even such an architect as his rival Bramante.

The *Last Supper* has undergone so many sacrilegious mutilations that it is, unfortunately, no longer possible to judge the original technical quality. The master made use of simple tones only but varied them agreeably. Most of the figures wear a red robe and a blue mantle, or "vice versa"; but among these we note yellow tunics, green mantles, green tunics, mantles of yellowish brown, a purplish tunic and mantle and here and there, a yellowish band or border, to relieve them. The costumes themselves are extremely simple, as we may suppose those of Christ and his disciples to have been. They consist of a toga, or, rather, a tunic, with closely fitting sleeves, but loose at the neck and leaving the throat bare; over this is thrown a full, flowing cloak; an uncut precious stone sometimes takes the place of a brooch or fibula and the bare feet are cased in sandals. Despite this severity, the draperies are cast with consummate knowledge and perfection. Those of the Saviour are especially ample and majestic. The tunic is displayed on the right breast and shoulder and the mantle is draped from the left shoulder across the body, enveloping all the rest of the figure in its folds.

In the *Last Supper* of the monastery of Santa Maria delle Grazie, painting triumphs over the final difficulties, resolves the final problems of aesthetics and of technique. Leonardo had realized his ideal, whether we judge of his work by its arrangement of line and mass, its colour, its movement, its treatment of drapery, or its dramatic expression. Alas! The master's triumph was short-lived. Incalculable disasters were soon to burst upon his protector and his fellow citizens.

Fortunately, he has left innumerable drawings to make up for the rarity of his pictures and these reveal the incomparable mastery, the incredible variety of the draughtsman in the most varied aspects. It is to this manifestation of his genius that I now propose to call attention.

Although the painter too often left his creations mere sketches, the draughtsman tried his hand at every process and excelled in all. We find him alternately making use of pen and ink, charcoal and silver-point, with equal mastery, the latter method being perhaps especially to his taste, because of the mysterious quality inherent in it.

After his establishment at Milan, he used red chalk, a more expeditious medium, which first appears in his studies for the *Last Supper*.

According to several critics (Emile Galichon, Morelli and Richter), one distinguishing characteristic of Leonardo's manner was his method of shading by means of parallel hatchings from left to right, a peculiarity explained by the fact that he was left-handed. But de Geymüller has shown this theory to be an exaggerated one.

In one single drawing (a study in the Louvre for the infant St John in the *Virgin of the Rocks),* the hatchings are laid in seven different directions; in the corner of the eye, they are laid one above the other in three directions.

A painter even more pre-eminently than a draftsman, Leonardo avoided over-definite contours in painting. He modelled with colour and with light rather than with lines and hatchings. Here he speaks for himself in saying that "on the beauty of faces do not make the lines of the muscles too insistent ('*con aspra definizione*'), but allow soft lights to melt gradually into pleasant and agreeable shades. This gives grace and beauty."

He recommends the use of the same colour for the contours as that used for the background – in other words, he deprecates the practice of separating the figures from the background by means of a dark outline.

To him, the chief triumph of painting lay in chiaroscuro and foreshortening: "*Il chiaro e lo scuro insieme co li scorti è la eccelenzia della scienza della pittura.*" He attached the utmost importance to relief and to the tactile quality of painting. Here he is at one with Michelangelo, who, in his letter to Varchi, pronounced painting to be excellent in proportion to the effect of relief it produces.

Lady with an Ermine (Portrait of Cecilia Gallerani), 1483-1490.
Oil on wood panel,
54.8 x 40.3 cm.
Muzeum Czartoryskich, Cracow.

It was, indeed, the human body in its most flexible aspect and still more the human soul in its most sensitive moods that he took as the basis and inspiration of his art. But it was the human body as a softly moulded mass, rather than as a bony, anatomical structure. In spite of his interest in anatomy, or rather myology, he had a horror of all things connected with death. No art was ever more radiant than his. From this sprang his distaste for architectural backgrounds. His independent genius rebelled against rigid stoical laws.

Leonardo looked at drawing from three points of view. First, he saw drawing as an art in itself – an end and not merely a means of practice. The elaboration of some of his portraits sufficiently proves this. His disinterestedness on this point was greater than that of Raphael, whose drawings are almost without exception sketches and cartoons for his pictures. Secondly, drawing was in Leonardo's eyes, a preliminary to the execution of pictures and statues; and thirdly, a kind of graphic commentary on, or necessary illustration of, his works. In the last case, drawing was to him merely a form of writing, a means of rendering his thought more clearly.

These rough sketches of his show the most admirable penetration and precision; they evoke the very essence of beings and of things. The most complex mechanisms become intelligible under Leonardo's pen or pencil.

The drawings for the *Battle of Anghiari*, especially those in the Turin Library, have a fire and vigor that is wanting in the drawings of the Florentine period and betray an intention on the part of the master to measure himself against Michelangelo.

The so-called *Caricatures* serve as pendants to these types of ideal beauty, making up a gallery of idiots and cretins, goitered, toothless, hare-lipped abortions, with noses and chins atrophied or developed to exaggeration. The artist who created the most perfect types of humanity also applied himself, long before Grandville and Caliot, to the reproduction of the most monstrous deformities; caricatures which show the intermediate degree between the man and the beast or, rather, man degraded below the level of the beast, by a hideous hybridism. In some examples, the nose is flattened, while the upper lip protrudes like those of the felidæ: in others, the nose is hooked and prominent as a parrot's beak.

The Sforza monument, unfinished though it was, had immediately given Leonardo a place in the front rank of sculptors, just as the *Last Supper* had raised him to the highest place among painters. Taking into account the scope and variety of his knowledge in the exact sciences, it was natural that the artist should have burned to try his hand at architecture.

An opportunity to experiment in this new domain soon presented itself. For years, the completion of the Milan cathedral had occupied the attention of all who were interested in gothic architecture. The master builders of Strasburg, as also Bramante, Francesco di Giorgio Martini and many others, had given advice and worked out plans.

In 1487 Leonardo, too, entered the lists in this great competition that stirred the enthusiasm of the last champions of the Middle Ages; he turned his attention to the cupola that was to crown the transept, the *"tiburium"*. Everything tends to prove that his design in the Gothic manner was rejected and henceforth the master's research was purely platonic.

Although we cannot positively attribute any existing building to Leonardo, it is easy to divine from his sketches what his designs may or would have been in stone. They would, firstly, have revealed the sense of harmony that characterized this purist *par excellence*, by the perfect equilibrium of the different parts of the edifice, attached to the central body by an absolutely organic and vital bond.

Leonardo the architect, like Leonardo the sculptor, had dreams of colossal, chimerical works. The riyal necropolis he planned was to consist, according to de Geymüller's calculations, of an artificial mountain, 600 meters in diameter at the base and of a circular temple, the pavement of which was to be on a level with the spires of Cologne Cathedral, while the interior was to be of the same width as the nave of St Peter's at Rome.

On another occasion, fired by the example of Aristotele di Fioravante, the famous Bolognese engineer, who had removed a tower from one place to another without demolishing it, he proposed to the Florentine government to raise the Baptistery by means of machinery and replace it on a base of steps. Needless to say, the project was not favourably received. Here again the great artist and scholar showed himself a visionary.

Portrait of a Musician, c. 1485.
Oil on wood panel, 43 x 31 cm.
Pinacoteca Ambrosiana, Milan.

III. ARTIST, THINKER AND MAN OF SCIENCE

Leonardo's Academy

Leonardo was not content only to create art; he had a strong desire to teach as well. In order to act more strongly on those by whom he was surrounded, he founded the academy that bore his name. This was not, as we might be tempted to think, merely an academic body devoted to the glorification of ability, or even an institution for public teaching. In all probability, it was a free society through which its members could obtain a more fruitful influence on each other and their neighbours by communication, by working together and by general community of tastes and studies.

It is generally agreed that the manuscripts left by Leonardo are fragments from his teaching in his Milanese academy.

From about his thirty-seventh year, according to Richter, Leonardo made it a habit to write down the results of his observations and continued to do so until his death, thus fulfilling to the end that duty of activity that is incumbent on every human creature. Even now, after great and irreparable losses his manuscripts and fragments of manuscripts reach a total of more than fifty and form more than five thousand pages of text.

It is important to address Leonardo's peculiar habit of writing in an Oriental fashion, from right to left. We know from the Uffizi drawing that he began the practice as early as 1473. Various pieces of evidence combine to show that his writing style was only one among several precautions taken against the pilfering of his secrets. He was in the habit of writing certain words in the form of anagrams, "Amor" for "Roma", "ilopan" for "Napoli."

From a palaeographic standpoint, the writing of Leonardo is still fifteenth-century in its character, in its smallness, and its rigidity as well as the shortness of its strokes above and below the line which differs essentially from the large and expressive writing of Michelangelo and Raphael.

During the thirty-five years that separate the first manuscript from the last, the writing undergoes no change whatsoever. The most we have acquired is the ability point to some slight differences between the characters used on the two early drawings of 1473 and 1478 and those that belong to his maturity or old age. Charles Ravaisson-Mollien has remarked that in his first attempts, Leonardo takes pleasure in forming elaborate letters, which he later on abandons for characters more suitable to a thinker and observer who wishes to lose no time in recording his experiences. In 1478, Leonardo is found experimenting with a sign resembling the beginning of a loop to take the place of *n;* later on, he nearly always reduces it to the simple stroke in common use.

Yet he presents a particular contradiction because his work is one long, consistent protest against formulae, against teaching, against tradition that pretends to instruct others on the treatment of a subject according to set and determined rules.

Like Leonardo's other works, the *Trattato della Pittura* still needs to be edited. It has not yet undergone the remodelling and coordination required to make it a real didactic treatise. The need of a sequence in the arrangement of its chapters and the innumerable repetitions show that it never received the master's last touches.

Though, imperfect as it is, it has never ceased to excite the keen interest of the artist and the amateur. Between 1651 and 1898, nearly thirty editions and translations have been published.

The treatise has been printed in two different forms. Firstly, there are the autographic fragments that are illustrated by numerous drawings by the master, which Richter was the first to publish. Secondly, there are several old copies that are more complete in some respects than the fragments. In these copies we recognize an effort of the disciples, if not to Leonardo himself, to create a due rearrangement.

As a result of Ludwig's research it has become known that the fragments of the *Trattato* printed by Richter form 662 paragraphs, while the Vatican MS runs to 944. The text of 225 paragraphs is identical both in the collected manuscripts and the Vatican copy.

The Vitruvian Man, 1490.
Pen and ink, 34.4 x 24.5 cm.
Galleria dell' Accademia, Venice.

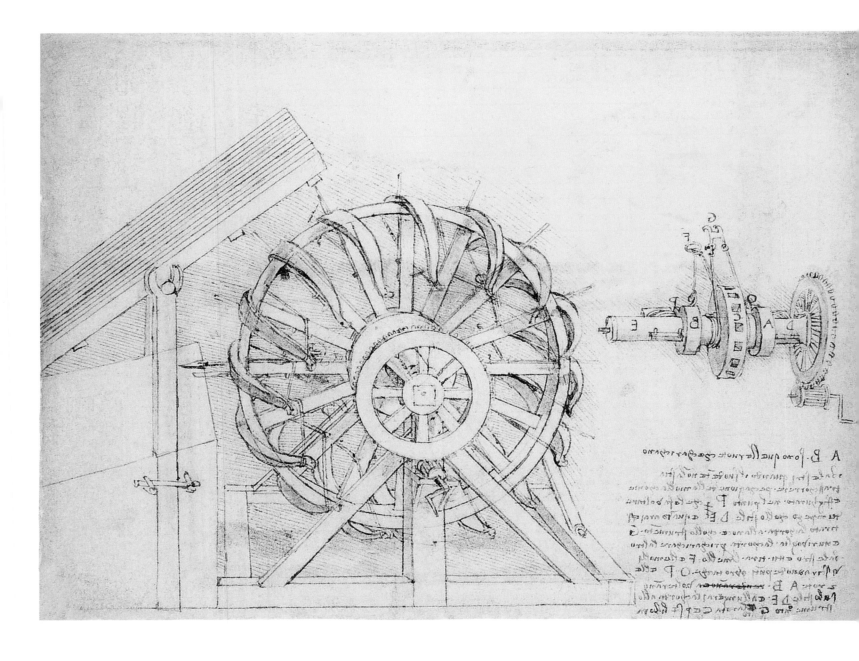

This great encyclopaedia of painting contains eight books: Poetry and Painting; Precepts for the Painter; Anatomy, Proportions; Drapery; Light and Shadow; Trees and Verdure; Clouds; and Horizon.

The major part of the book is devoted to a comparison of painting with poetry *"Sicut pictura poesis"*.

The more or less prominent question was whether painting was superior to sculpture, or vice versa, which was a topic passionately discussed throughout the Renaissance. Half a century before Leonardo, Leone Battista Alberti had concluded in favour of painting.

As Leonardo in the *Trattato* never wearies of asserting that the painter should be universal and we have every right to believe that the teaching he gave was encyclopaedic.

No artist's eye has seen more profoundly than his into the mysteries of light; no artist's brain has more clearly formulated its rules. Inside da Vinci painter and optician were combined as the result of innumerable experiments. Nothing escaped him – sunlight effects, rain effects, effects of mist and dust, variations of the atmosphere. He investigated the changes undergone by the tones of nature by watching them through coloured glasses.

War Machine with Sixteen Catapults, c. 1485.
Pen and ink, 22 x 30 cm.
Biblioteca Ambrosiana, Milan.

The book devoted to light and shadow is of peculiar subtlety. Only the eye of Leonardo could distinguish so many different shades:

"There are three kinds of shadows. One kind is produced by a single point of light, such as the sun, the moon, or a flame. The second is produced by a door, a window, or other opening

through which a large part of the sky can be seen. The third is produced by such a universal light as the illumination of our hemisphere when the sun is not shining."

The teaching of perspective occupies a large section of the *Trattato*. Leonardo divides it into three types: "Linear perspective (*prospettiva liniale*), color perspective and aerial perspective otherwise called the diminution in the distinctness of bodies, the diminution of their size and the diminution of their colour. The first has its origin in the eye, the two others in the veil of air interposed between the eye and the object."

Long before Albrecht Dürer, to whom the invention of the *camera lucida* is usually ascribed, the Florentine master contrived an easy way of drawing figures in perspective with the help of a sheet of glass. He describes the process in the *Codex Atlanticus and* in the *Trattato*.

The author of the *Trattato* devoted much study to the preparation of different pigments. Unfortunately, the results of these investigations are now in a very fragmented condition.

We have seen that fresco did not appeal to him. On the other hand, unlike Michelangelo, he was passionately attached to the oil medium. He was the first to win a full harmony and transparency of tone to obtain the effects of chiaroscuro which even now, after four centuries have passed, still transport us with admiration. But these "tours de force" were dearly bought. The master demanded more from oil painting than it could give. He applied it indifferently to easel pictures and to monumental wall paintings. The *Last Supper,* the *Virgin of the Rocks,* the *Belle Ferronière and* the *Mona Lisa* are all in a sad state; such as are not blackened are covered with cracks.

Mechanism for Alternative to Continuous Movement, c. 1485. Pen and ink, 27.8 x 38.5 cm. Biblioteca Ambrosiana, Milan.

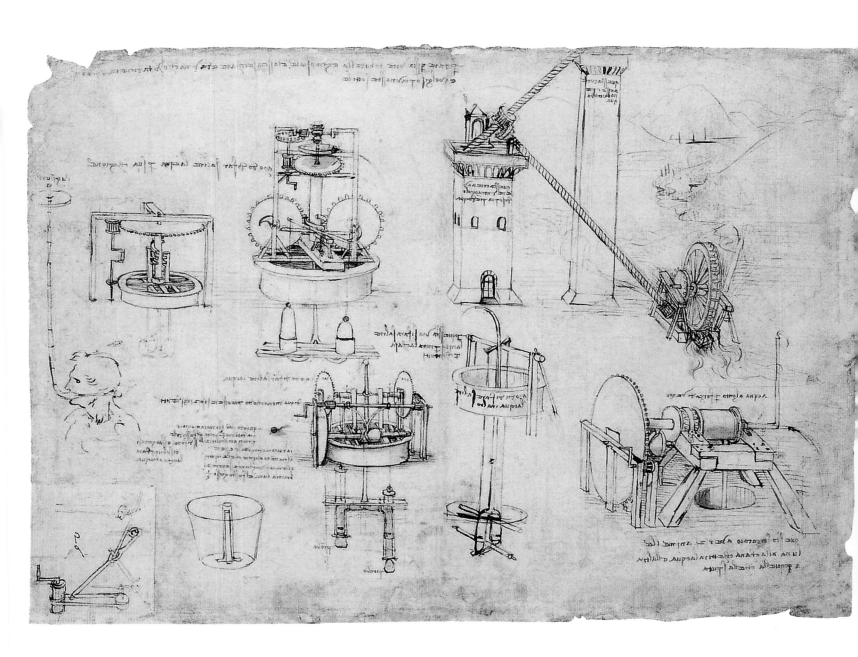

Hydrotechnical Mechanisms and Studies, c. 1480.
Pen and ink, 39.7 x 28.5 cm.
Biblioteca Ambrosiana, Milan.

Hydrotechnical Studies, c. 1480.
Pen and ink, 39.7 x 28.5 cm.
Biblioteca Ambrosiana, Milan.

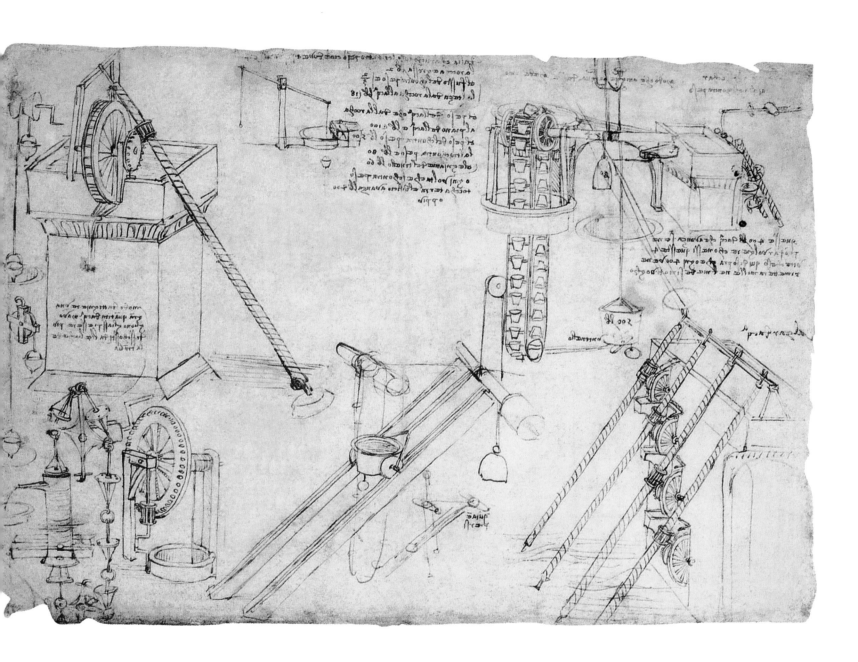

*Studies of a Flying Machine with
a Mechanism Activated by Feet
and Hands*, c. 1487-1490.
Pen and ink, 23.2 x 16.7 cm.
Bibliothèque de l'Institut de
France, Paris.

*Flying Machine with Half-fixed
Wings*, c. 1488-1490.
Pen and ink, red chalk,
29 x 20.5 cm.
Biblioteca Ambrosiana, Milan.

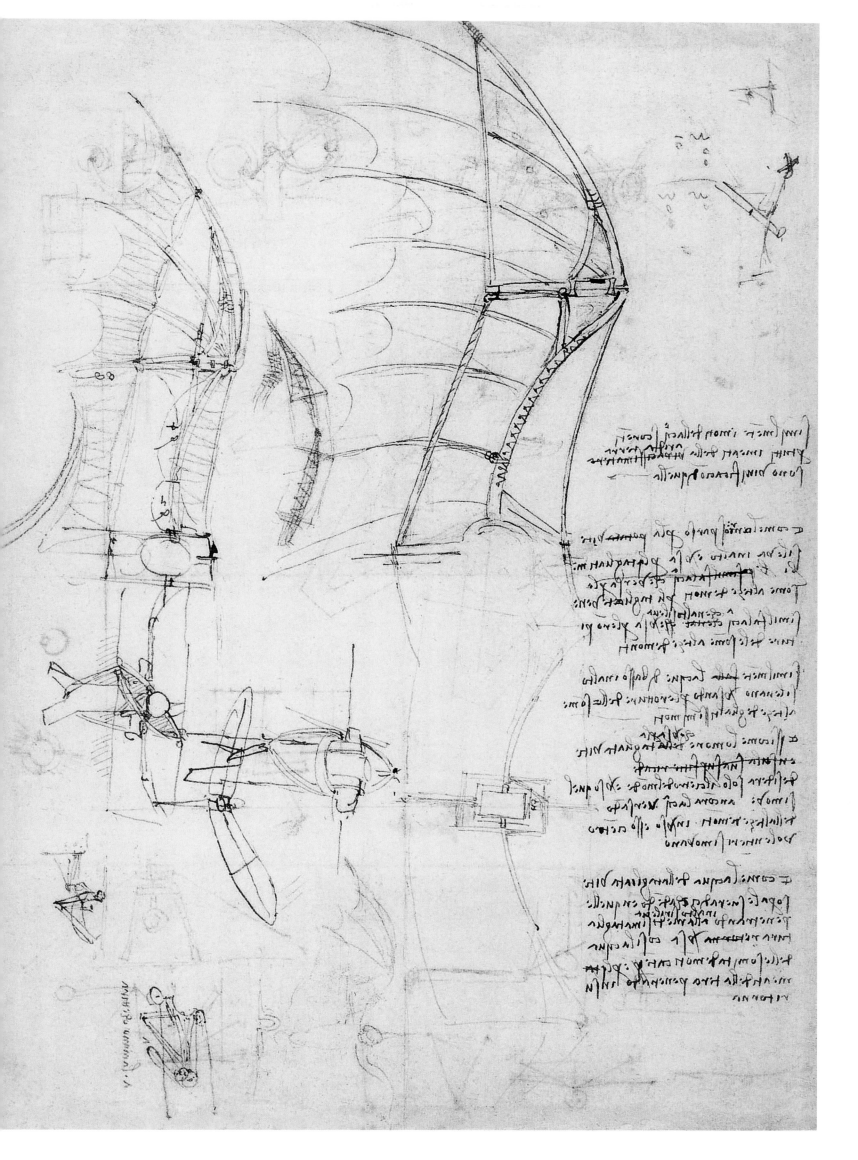

de lionardo Vinci

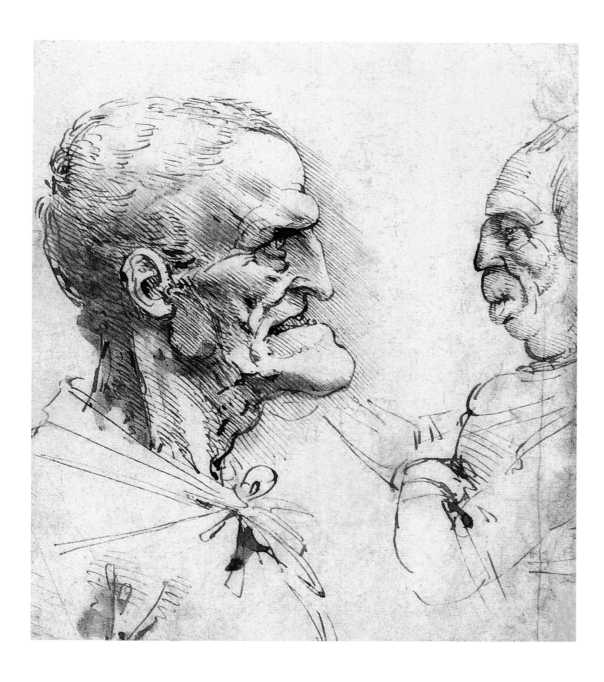

Landscapes took over the thoughts of Leonardo. His oldest dated drawing – an alpine view – bears witness to the efforts he made in that direction, even in his youth! In the *Trattato* he often reverts to the subject. According to him landscapes should be represented so that the trees are half in light, half in shadow, but the best way is to paint them when the sun is hidden by clouds so that the trees may be illuminated by the general light of the sky and shadowed by the universal shadow of the earth. "And these," he adds, "will be most obscure in the parts nearest to the centre of the tree and to the earth."

His studies of proportion and movement of the human figure were intended to complete the *Trattato*. For the most part this research was carried out between the years 1489 and 1498. in 1498, Pacioli notes the completion of Leonardo's work in the dedication to his own *De divina Proportione* ("*Leonardo da Vinci... havenda già con tutta diligentia al degno libro de pictura e movimento humani posto fine*").

Naturally enough, Leonardo made use of the labors of his Greek and Roman predecessors. However, on one occasion his taking count of antique opinions was ill inspired. Basing himself on Vitruvius, he adopted eight heads, or ten faces, as the normal height of the human figure. Now this calculation is false. Modern science has proved that the normal height equals seven and a half heads, or, at most, seven and three quarters.

We see, then, that the *Trattato della Pittura* forms a perpetual commentary on the artistic activity of Leonardo. It is a collection of subtle ideas and practical counsels, of scientific

Grotesque Profile of a Man,
c. 1485-1490.
Pen and ink, 12.6 x 10.4 cm.
Biblioteca Ambrosiana, Milan.

Portraits of Two Men,
c. 1487-1490.
Pen and ink, 16.3 x 14.3 cm.
Royal Library, Windsor Castle.

observations in which the spirit of analysis is pushed to its extreme limits and of those concrete guesses or intuitions that reveal the artist of genius. In spite of the occasional minuteness of its instructions, it is better fitted to stimulate the mind than to act as a practical guide and formulary.

In its great suggestiveness, it is addressed rather to those artists who love to think for themselves than to those who are content to accept ready-made formulae. It must be confessed that no school has felt its inspiration less than that formed by Leonardo himself, whose immediate pupils – Boltraffio, Marco d'Oggiono, Salai, Melzi – never allowed any hard thinking to disturb their equanimity.

We must not forget, however, that in Leonardo's studio, theoretical teaching was always supplemented by practical and direct oral instruction.

The master took pupils, or rather apprentices, to live in his house. His "terms" were five lire a month, a very modest sum when we remember all the discomforts and responsibilities that then attended the taking of apprentices.

To hear what Leonardo says of the troubles this system brought upon him confirms what we already know of his placidity: "Giacomo came to live with me on the feast of St Mary Magdalen in 1490. He was ten years old. The second day, I ordered two shirts, a pair of hose and a doublet for him. When I put aside the money to pay for these things, he took it out of my purse; I was never able to make him confess the robbery, although I was certain of it. A thieving, lying, pig-headed glutton. The next day I supped with Giacomo Andrea and the said Giacomo; he ate for two and did mischief for four, for he broke three flasks and upset the wine and then came and supped where I was.

"Item: on the 7 September he stole a stylus worth 22 soldi from Marco's studio, while he (Marco) was with me; afterwards, the said Marco, after a long search, found it hidden in the said Giacomo's box. Lira 1, soldi 2. Item: on the 26 January following, while I was with Messer Galeazzo da San Severino arranging his joust and while certain footmen were undressing in order to try on some costumes of savages in which they had to appear, Giacomo crept near the wallet of one of them, which was lying on the bed with other effects and stole a few coppers which he found in it. Lire 2, soldi 4.

"Item: Messer Agostino da Pavia having given me, in the said house, a Turkish skin to make a pair of shoes, this Giacomo stole it before the month was out and sold it to a cobbler for 20 soldi and, as he himself confessed to me, bought sweetmeats with the money. Lire, 2. Item: on 2 April, Gian-Antonio left a silver stylus lying on one of his drawings and Jacopo stole it; it was worth 24 soldi. Lira 1, soldi 4."

Certain other pupils of Leonardo's, besides Salai, Melzi, Marco d'Oggiono and Boltraffio, to whom I shall return later, are known to us by the master's autograph notes or by other documentary evidence. Among them were one Galeazzo (1494), mentioned only by name; two Germans: Julio Tedesco, who entered the studio 16 March 1493 and Gorgio Tedesco (1504-1515); finally one Lorenzo (1505), aged seventeen.

The Florentine Riccio della Porta della Croce and the Spaniard Ferrando were two of the master's assistants when he was working on the *Battle of Anghiari*.

Leonardo was not fortunate enough to have an entourage of engravers around him, like the band who worked for Raphael under the direction of Marc Antonio. But indeed his compositions, so much less literary than those of Raphael, could not have failed to lose enormously in reproduction. Their beauty lay mainly in the suavity of expression, the delicacy of modelling and charm of colour. If the rude and monotonous processes of early Italian engraving sufficed, as Émile Galichon has happily said, for the rendering of Mantegna's austerity and Botticelli's somewhat acrid beauty, "it was powerless as yet to translate the indescribable grace of Leonardo's women. Hence it was that Leonardo and his pupils used the burine merely by way of experiment."

Only five or six early engravings of the *Last Supper* have survived and they are by anonymous hands. The *Madonnas,* the *St John,* the *Battle of Anghiari and* the portraits first engaged the attention of engravers at a comparatively late period.

The *Trattato* contains a passage that gives an instructive glimpse into the studio of Leonardo. The painter, we are told, sits comfortably before his work and drives his brush with its load

Frontal Study of a Naked Man,
c. 1503-1509.
Pen and ink, 23.6 x 14.6 cm.
Royal Library, Windsor Castle.

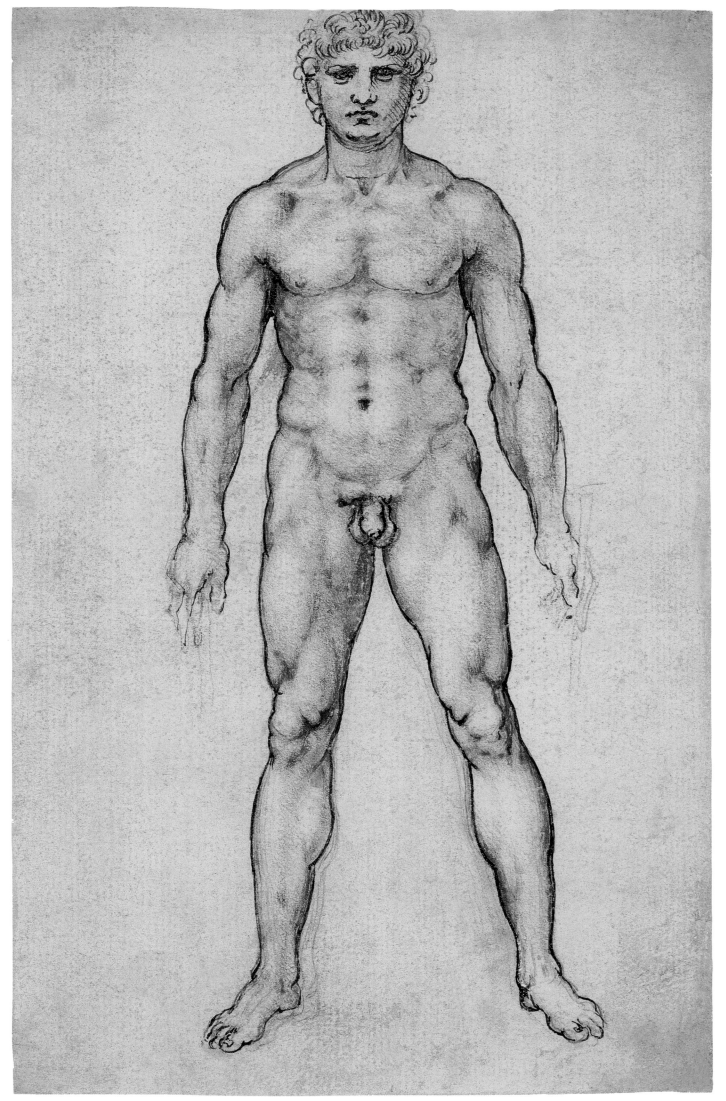

71

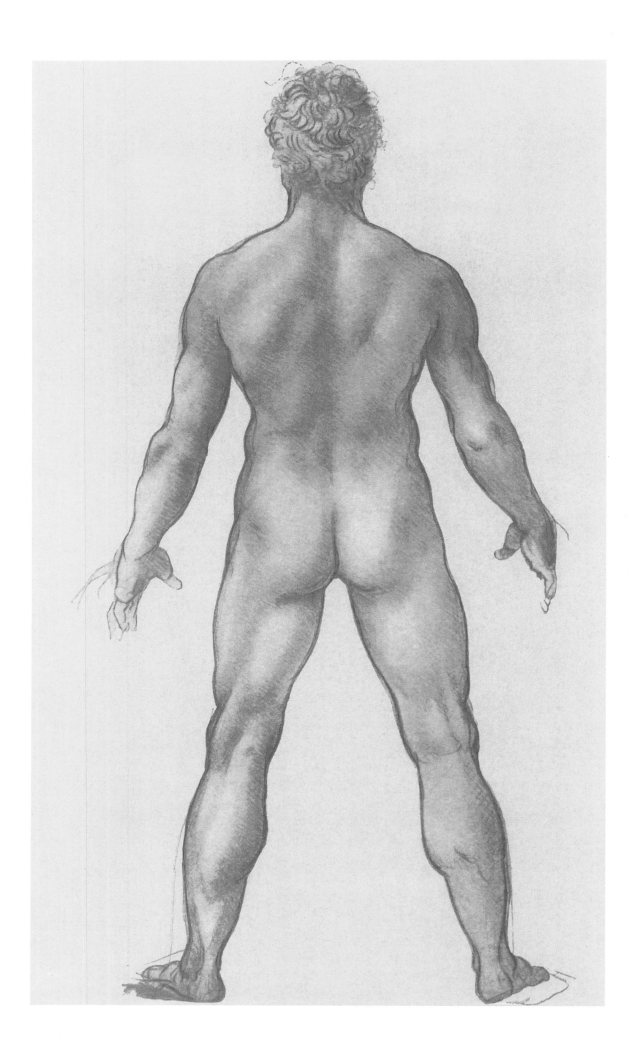

of beautiful colour into his easel. He always dressed to please himself. His dwelling was clean and neat and full of fine pictures. He often had musicians to keep him company, or readers who would recite works of literature to the delight of those present.

Leonardo's Dealings with the Antique

The initial stage of Leonardo's career coincides with the last supreme encounter between the ancient tradition (the tradition of the Middle Ages) and the new spirit of the times. Down to about the third quarter of the fifteenth century painting, if we exclude the painting of the school of Padua, had sought inspiration from Roman models for costume details or simply ornamental details. Now, taking examples from the other arts of architecture and sculpture, it strove to assimilate the actual principles and the very essence of classic art. Botticelli, Ghirlandajo and, above all, Filippino Lippi exerted themselves unceasingly to build up their frescos or pictures on the teachings offered to them by an army of statues, some specimen of which came to light each day under the pickaxe of the excavator. These efforts, rudimentary enough at first, culminated some years later in the triumph of classicism under the banner of Raphael and his disciples.

How did Leonardo understand and how did he account for this factor that became more and more difficult to neglect, a factor which spread itself over the intellectual life of the 'quattrocentisti' by so many ramifications?

At first glance, one is inclined to deny that Leonardo ever felt the influence of classic models. "He alone," states Eugène Piot, "was the true faultless painter. The study of nature, untrammeled by absorption in classic ideals, a constant and unremitting study, carried on always and everywhere, with a perseverance and tenacity peculiar to himself that had revealed to him all the secrets of power in art, all the mysteries of grandeur and physical beauty."

Leonardo had too fine a taste to allow the introduction into the art of painting effects proper to sculpture, as the great Andrea Mantegna was doing at the same time. It is because of this particular reason that he did not believe that a painter would profit by the imitation of antique statues. However, these opinions are more or less superficial.

A careful study of da Vinci's work leads us to the inevitable conclusion that whatever he may have said about antiquity and however completely he may have avoided dependence upon it, he was well acquainted with it in practice and had assimilated its spirit.

He only permitted the use of the ancient orders, except occasionally he would allow a combination with the Byzantine cupola. He accepted the authority of Vitruvius, a mentor to which he was constantly referring.

Many of his designs are reproductions or at least resemble Greek and Roman monuments, notably the Mausoleum of Halicarnassus; one of his ideas for the base of the Sforza statue was taken from the castle of St Angelo at Rome.

The mere fact that Leonardo accepted Roman forms in architecture tends to prove that he admired classic methods in architectural settings and in the arrangement of figures in that specific setting. The principles of grouping that he followed in the Sforza statue, in his *Last Supper*, the *Saint Anne* are in no way inconsistent with those of antique models.

The attention Leonardo gave to the nude is also attributed to his study of the antique. Every now and again, especially in his sketches for the *Adoration of the Magi*, he drew figures unclothed so that he could better observe their structure and their movements. What simplicity in his composition! What rigor in his selection! What thoroughness and completeness in his synthesis!

The young painter had little interest in realism concerning costume. Living in an ideal world, the popular culture of his time did not concern him, so it's very rare to find memoranda of actual life in his work. No other artist has shown less solicitude in those directions. He was interested in man himself and not in man's historical setting.

Leonardo's proscription of the costume of his own time, a costume reproduced with so much care by the "quattrocentisti" was, like the retrospective nature of his investigations, proof of his abstract and idealistic mind. Putting aside a few portraits, the figures he painted are clothed in

A Nude Man from behind,
c. 1504-1506.
Red chalk, 27 x 16 cm.
Royal Library, Windsor Castle.

attire from Antiquity; they wear tunics, togas, cloaks; and wear them with an ease that justifies the fact that no artist has at one time modernized and preserved the noble simplicity of the antique costume so successfully as the author of the *Last Supper* and the *Mona Lisa*.

Leonardo declared in the *Trattato* that the representation of contemporary fashions should be avoided as much as possible (*"fugire il più che si può gli abiti deila sua età"*), except in the case of funerary statues.

He was Greek in his love for those androgynous forms, uniting masculine vigor with feminine grace which played a large a part in his most complete work, *St John the Baptist* located in the Louvre.

Although he used details from his Greek and Roman predecessors, Leonardo had no desire to tie himself to their chariot cart wheels. This is easily seen from the way which he treated iconography, allegory and kindred subjects. No artist has ever pushed independence further than da Vinci. It could be said that he pushed it too far because in matters like these it is absolutely necessary that a painter be in sympathetic with his public, a result only appears after deferring to tradition, or by extraordinary proselytizing efforts on his own part. However, Leonardo followed neither course and many of his conceptions would be quite incomprehensible without the help of the explanations he left to us.

Rejecting all but a few of the traditional attributes (a column for Courage, three eyes for Prudence and so on), he started to create his own complete symbolism. He proposed to represent Fame in the shape of a bird covered with tongues instead of feathers, to place in the hand of Ingratitude a burning brand, suggesting the wood that nourishes a fire but is itself consumed.

After all this, We must discuss in detail the question of Leonardo's imitations of the antique. They are vastly more numerous than is generally assumed and in many definite points they corroborate the general view put forward here.

Take sculpture for example, it is not proven that Leonardo made any use of the colossal horses of the Quirinal in Rome – one of the drawings in the Resta collection at the Ambrosiana is certainly not by him – on the other hand, I am certainly inclined to maintain that he studied the famous antique equestrian group in bronze, at Pavia: *"Di quel di Pavia si lauda più il movimento che nessun altra cosa."*

Where did Leonardo get the idea of rearing horses? No doubt it came from Antiquity. We may easily convince ourselves of this by examining gems representing such things as the fall of Phaeton, the death of Hector and the death of Hippolytus.

Turning now to painting, we may point out that besides the more or less veiled reminiscences already alluded to there are a certain number of textual imitations. In his studies for the *Last Supper*, the apostle in profile recalls in the most striking manner the Roman medallions of the time of the Antonines, notably those of Lucius Verus.

His *St John the Baptist*, in the Louvre, is clearly based on certain antique types, half masculine and half feminine, such as the Apollino, the Bacchus and the Hermaphroditus and yet the combination is completely reminiscent of Leonardo.

To conclude, this great artist treated the antique as it should be treated by one who wishes to profit by its teaching and desires to receive lessons rather than labour-saving formula. After long and thoughtful study, Leonardo mastered the antique spirit, allowing it to radiate freely within him. He counted upon the wealth and independence of his own nature to enable him to turn it to his own use, to transform it and to produce with its aid works of art which should be essentially vital and modern.

The Muscles and Bones of the Leg and Hip, Comparative Study of Skeletons of Man and Horse, c. 1506-1508. Pen and ink with red chalk on red background, 28.5 x 20.5 cm. Royal Library, Windsor Castle.

The Poet, the Thinker and the Man of Science

The painter of the *Mona Lisa* and the *Last Supper* enchanted and dazzled his contemporaries at first glance and after four centuries his popularity has not diminished the prestige of his artistic creations. As a thinker and investigator he was less fortunate. It required the efforts of several generations of learned men, from Venturi, Libri and Govi,

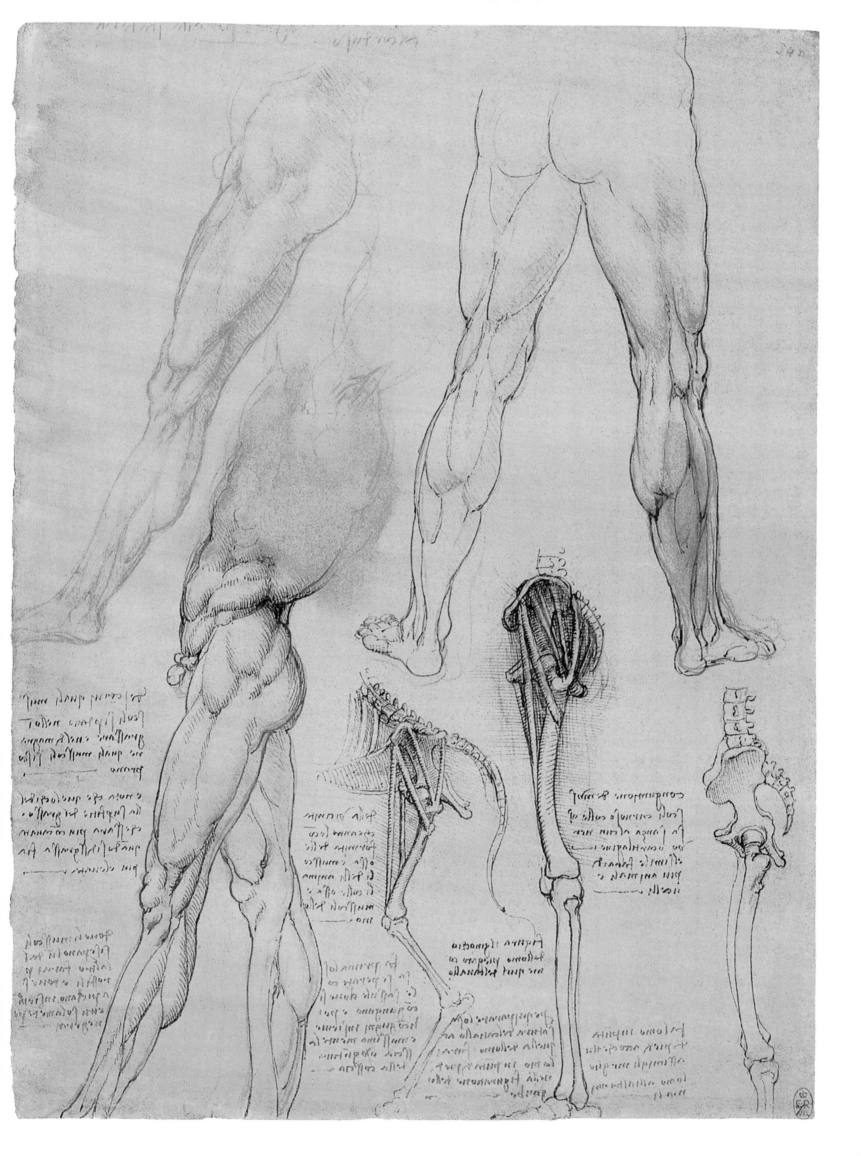

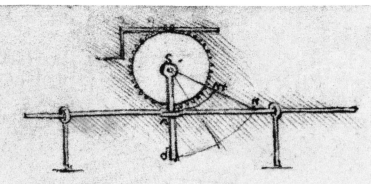

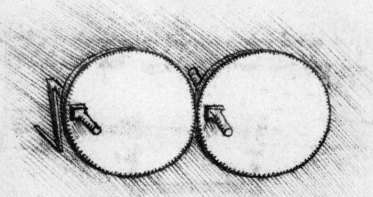

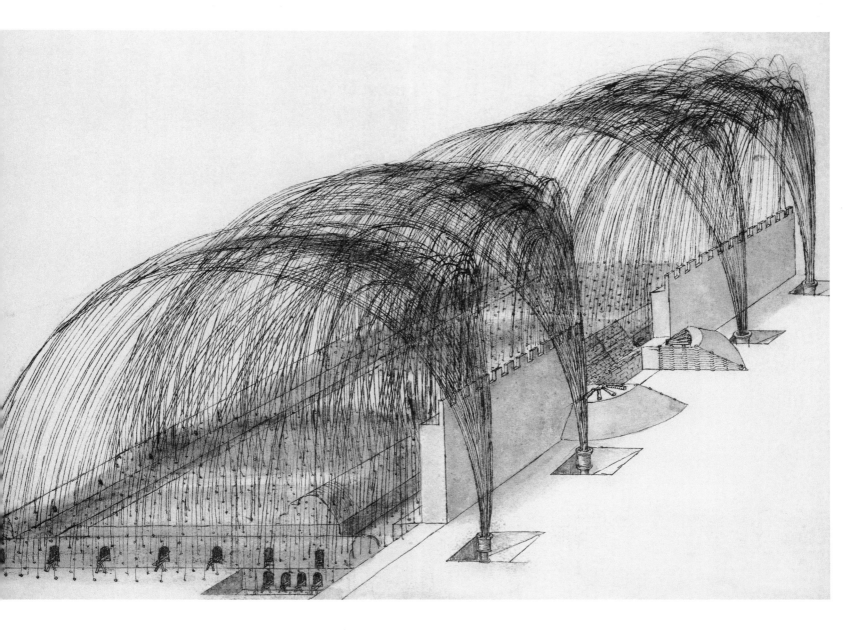

down to Uzielli, Richter, Ravaisson-Mollien, Beltrami and Piumati to complete the work of rehabilitation.

I also propose to investigate how letters were integrated into his genius.

To form an accurate judgment of Leonardo's writings we must begin by recognizing that here we have to deal, in literature and philosophy no less than in science, with a self-taught man. Education had little effect on nature's endowments on the artist and we may safely assert that the education received by this particular child of genius in the small town of Vinci and afterwards in Florence was in a word careless. We can, moreover, point to evidence on Leonardo's early studies that bears every sign of authenticity. A biographer tells us that he showed an unbounded, even extravagant, thirst for acquiring knowledge, but that his curiosity was equalled by the instability of his tastes. He passed from arithmetic to music, from natural history to the arts of design and from these to the occult sciences without any sign of fatigue, but also without any steady devotion. His literary and historical studies were always in second place.

In his later years Leonardo attempted to fill the gaps in his education. He applied himself more particularly to the study of Latin. Here he had to learn everything. If we may judge from the glossary he prepared for his own use, he had not even acquired the rudiments when he was some thirty-five or forty years old. He found it necessary to write down the meaning of such elementary pronouns, adverbs, conjunctions and prepositions as *"sed, aliquid, quid, instar, tunc, praeter"*.

It is a little surprising to find the literary element holding such an important place in the studies of Leonardo; Ovid, Dante, Petrarch, stand side by side with Poggio, Philelpho, Burchiello and Pulci. Philosophy occupies as large a place as poetry. The titles of his books and the names of the authors he honored – Albertus Magnus, Diogenes Laertius, Platina,

Studies of the Transmission of Strength and of the Lifting of a Beam,1493-1497.
Pen and ink, 21.3 x 15 cm.
Biblioteca Nacional, Madrid.

Mortars Bombarding a Fortress, c. 1503-1504.
Pen, ink and brown wash over black chalk.
Royal Library, Windsor Castle.

Study for a Fortified Mechanism with Two Gaps, 1504-1508.
Pen and ink, wash, 44 x 29 cm.
Biblioteca Ambrosiana, Milan.

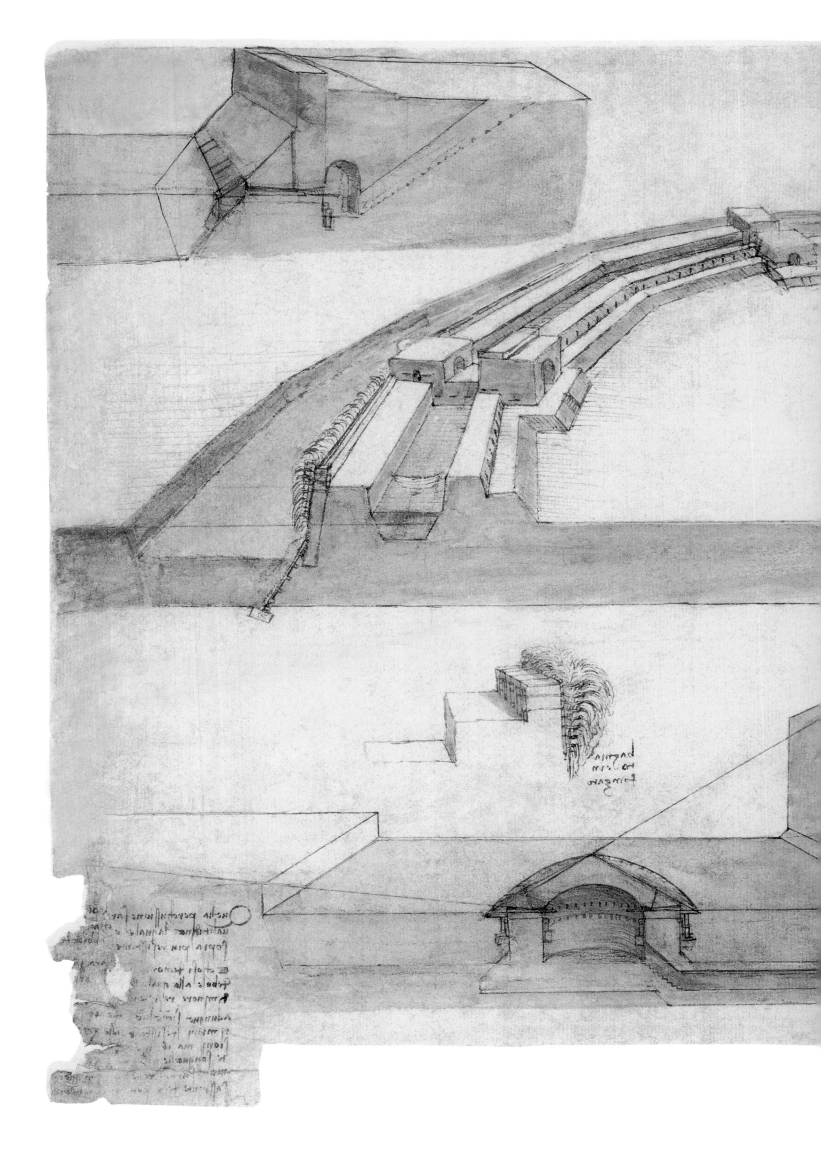

Marsilio Ficino – prove the eclecticism and liberality of their possessor. Religion and morals are not forgotten; they are represented by the *Bible,* the *Psalms, Æsop,* the *Flowers of Virtue;* the champions of history are Livy, Justinian and the chronicler Isidorus. Special treatises on arithmetic, cosmography, medicine, anatomy, agriculture and the military arts complete Leonardo's library. The section devoted to natural history is remarkable; it includes the works of Pliny, John de Mandeville and a *Lapidarium,* that is to say, compilations in which romance fills as large a space as science.

Leonardo more than made up for his lack of education by his natural talents. His contemporaries agree in declaring that he was the best *improvisatore* of his time: *"il migliore dicitore di rime all' improviso del tempo."* The five thousand pages of manuscript he left us do not contain the slightest implication of a love affair. It seems that he lived for art and science and, though a brother of Faust, no Marguerite ever hung upon his neck to distract or console him.

In regards to his poetry, if the fine conciseness and stirring eloquence of Michelangelo are absent, we find instead a great wealth of imagery and the art of rendering in words the effects that had previously been confined to painting. Everything in them is sincerely felt and observed–qualities that are too rare in the refined and artificial literature of sixteenth-century Italy to be passed over in silence.

Side by side with the poet we find the moralist and thinker.

Richter hypothesized that at some point in his life Leonardo converted to Islam. Lets dig deeper, with the help of his writings and of certain characteristic features of his career, to determine what Leonardo's religious convictions really were.

To begin with, even if it could be shown – and this is precisely one of the points most in dispute – that Leonardo had broken with the teachings of the Catholic Church, it would still be nonetheless certain that he was a deist and not an atheist or materialist.

Doubts of Leonardo's orthodoxy are very old. As early as the middle of the sixteenth century, Vasari spoke of his *"capricci nel filosafar delle cose naturale"*, adding that the author of the *Last Supper* "had taken up such heretical notions that he really belonged to no religion and, in short, that he laid more store by his quality as a philosopher than as a Christian." However, on a more careful examination the biographer seems to have recognized the slight foundation upon which his assertions rested because he left them out of his second edition which was published in 1588.

Leonardo over and over again reverts to the benevolence and grandeur of the Supreme Being and always names him with emotion. He celebrates the justice of the Creator, of the *"primo motore"* who had willed that no force should lack the necessary qualities for the work it had to do.

To understand such a state of mind we must place ourselves at the point of view from the Italy of the Renaissance and take account the indolence, the *"vis inertiæ"*, which led thinkers and scholars as well as artists to respect religious things. Like his contemporaries, Leonardo bows before the dogmas taught to him during his childhood. "I leave on one side," he states, "the sacred writings, seeing that they are supreme truth" *(lascio star le lettere incoronate, perche sono sommo verità).*

When, throughout his studies, he is driven to choose between accepted beliefs and the conclusions to which his investigations lead, he dismisses all but the truth from his mind. The Church teaches that the world was created 5,288 years before the birth of Christ, but Leonardo counts by hundreds of thousands of years and he agrees that the visible action of the Po upon the valley through which it flows must have required two thousand centuries.

Leonardo's research in geology led him to touch upon the gravest problems of Biblical history: for example, Noah's flood— was it a universal flood or was it not?

Let's turn to the attitude of Leonardo towards Christianity. We cannot doubt that, although he respected the beliefs in which he had been brought up (as his proceedings with regard to the *Last Supper,* his scruples in completing the figure of Christ; his conversation with Zenale show), the founder of the Milanese Academy portrays a certain independence of mind and shows that he attached more importance to works than to dogmas.

Study of Shields and Explosion of a Bomb, c. 1485-1488. Pen and ink, 20 x 27.3 cm. Ecole Nationale Supérieure des Beaux-Arts, Paris.

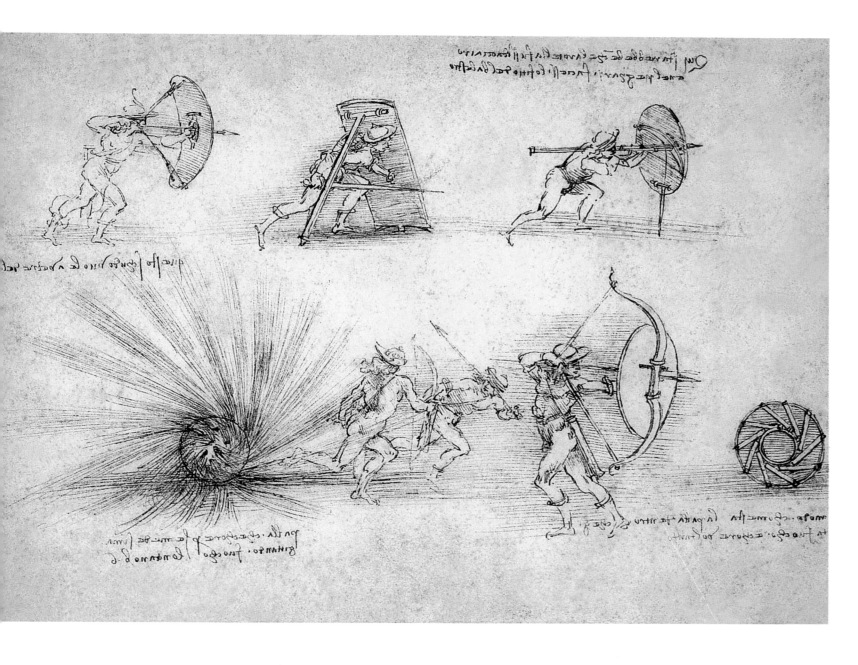

81

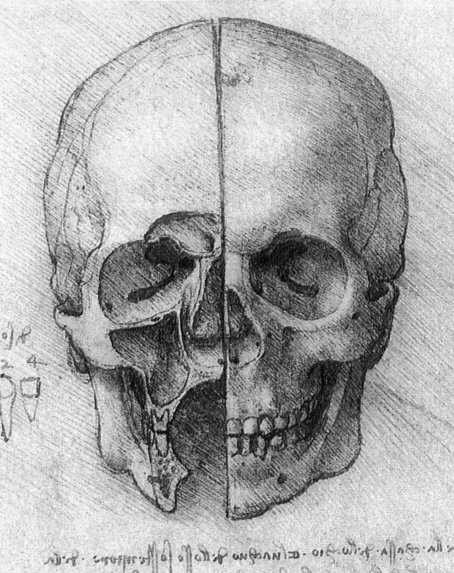

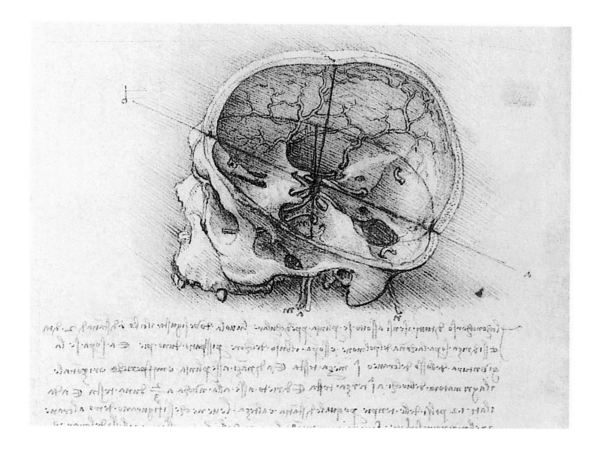

The seventy seventh section of the *Trattato* is devoted to discussing the observation of saints' days. Leonardo was severe upon hypocrites and does not hesitate to show us that, in his opinion, the spirit is vastly more important than the letter in matters of religion.

Leonardo embraced a certain prejudice against the "typical" clergy. Like so many upright natures, he inclined to misanthropy as time went on, until, in the end, bitterness took the place of serenity.

It is obvious from all these different pieces of evidence that Leonardo, without displaying any special marks of devotion or taking part in theological discussions, submitted with docility to the demands of public religion, as, in fact, every one who did not wish to become acquainted with the stake had to do. Nevertheless, it was conduct that might have been the result of calculation that sprang from within him, from the tolerance we look for in all superior minds.

Leonardo's pictures and drawings allow us to see a little deeper into the problem. They show that except in his rendering of the *Last Supper*, he took greater liberties with sacred iconography than any other artist did. Not content with suppressing the nimbi and other traditional attributes of holiness, he represents the actors in their sacred history in attitudes which, though full of poetry and tenderness, are inconsistent with the terrible mysteries of religion, for example, the Divine Child teasing a lamb or a cat, the Virgin sitting on her mother's knees and so on. Yet, according to his contemporaries, the pictures of Leonardo seemed inspired with the purest and most profound religious sentiment.

Leonardo's theories had a tendency to lean towards transcendental philosophy, because he taught that our bodies are in subjection to heaven and heaven is in subjection to the spirit. It is difficult to evolve any type of system from a collection of floating and contradictory assertions. He succeeds in defining the spirit as "power mingled with the body, because the power is unable to govern itself alone or even move in any way and if you say that it does govern itself, that is impossible in the midst of the elements, for if the spirit is an incorporeal quantity, such a quantity is called a vacuum and a vacuum does not exist in nature.

Yet the glory of Leonardo has a peculiarity and no other creative genius of our own time can compare to. If the study of his manuscripts enables us to antedate by two, or occasionally three or four, centuries many capital discoveries, the rights of his successors remain none the less intact. This requires explanation. Leonardo's manuscripts remained unpublished until within the last few years, so that the laws he established or at least divined had all to be independently rediscovered.

The Skull Sectioned, 1489.
Pen and ink, 19 x 13.3 cm.
Royal Library, Windsor Castle.

A Cranium Sectioned, 1489.
Pen and ink, 19 x 13.7 cm.
Royal Library, Windsor Castle.

Map of the Imola City, c. 1502.
Pen and ink, tempera,
44 x 60.2 cm.
Royal Library, Windsor Castle.

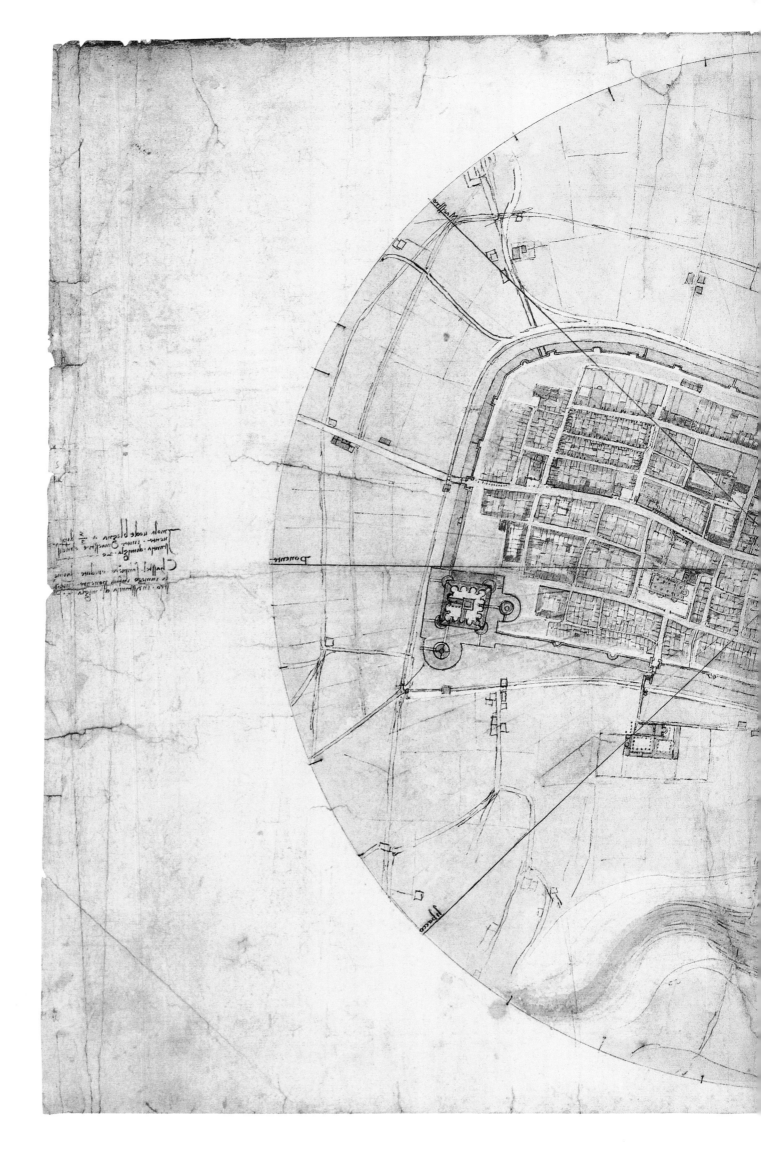

Indeed, it is impossible to acquit Leonardo of blame in this connection. Did he think himself immortal? At the age of sixty, he had taken no measures for the publication of his works. He paid dearly for his negligence. It is evident that his strength of character was not equal to his loftiness of intellect. We need not be surprised to find that it has been left to the nineteenth century to do tardy justice to the man of genius who divined a whole world of fundamental truth.

An alliance between art and science was not a new idea in Italy. Minds trained in the incomparable gymnasium of classic education and could attack the most arduous tasks without danger of a check. In such an enterprise the painter of the *Last Supper* and the sculptor of the Sforza statue could be justified by the example of many famous Italians. Brunellesco had been an ardent student of mathematics; Piero della Francesca of geometry; Alberti had composed the *Ludi Matematici* and invented a way of measuring the depth of the sea in places where lead could not be used; he had also busied himself with – *"de motibus ponderis"* – the movements of weights.

Was Leonardo's strong interest in scientific research a help, or a hindrance to him as an artist? He has often been cited as an example of the possibilities of combining art and science; a genius whose analytic faculties and reason were reinforced by imagination and emotion. But was this the case? Harassed by his perpetual desire to investigate, Leonardo's inspiration was ignited at every moment. No artist hesitated more; none has left more unfinished masterpieces. It was his scientific interests, too, which made him seek the solution of the laws of chiaroscuro and brown tonalities (to the detriment of that splendor of colour revealed by the Venetians).

All evidence is unanimous in showing that as a child he had a gift for the exact sciences. His entry into Verrocchio's studio confirmed these abilities, which, in him, were combined with an irresistible predilection for art. We know that Verrocchio was a passionate student of geometry and perspective, but whatever he may have done for his pupil, the latter was, above all things, the master of his own work.

Living in northern Italy was like leaven for bread in the case of Leonardo; it was contact with the Milanese that drew out his scientific potential. His new fellow-citizens had neither the lofty culture of the Florentines nor their spiritual aspirations. They adhered, in fact, to doctrines diametrically opposed to those of the Tuscans. To the altar of Plato they opposed that of Aristotle and of Avicenna and Averroes, his Arab interpreters. In the seventeenth century these leaders still counted numerous followers among the professors of Pavia, Padua and Bologna. They were, if I am not mistaken, the true initiators of Leonardo. They taught him to observe as well as to reflect and to alternate experiments with abstract thinking. Their disciple, independent as he was, constantly invoked their evidence, while careful not to expose their errors.

In the exact sciences, classical antiquity was by no means the only source of progress. It was through Leonardo Pisano, called Fibonacci, the greatest mathematician of the Middle Ages, that major innovations were being made.

Of this Leonardo affords a striking proof. He consults the ancients, but in the right sceptical spirit, accepting their discoveries when they seem to him well founded (what scientist could do otherwise?) but never hesitating to set them aside when experience shows them to be mistaken.

From first to last our hero lived in a strange and compromising world, but this fact has escaped those who have wished to turn him into a sort of Mahatma. Just as Christ frequented publicans, so did da Vinci take pleasure in the society of mystics, astrologers, alchemists and charlatans of every kind.

His baptism in all this was received in Florence from Marsilio Ficino, the favorite philosopher of the Medici family and the great propagandist of the Platonic philosophy. We know that in his little collection of books the future painter of the *Last Supper* and the *Mona Lisa* possessed Ficino's treatise on the *Immortalità d' Anima,* of which a Latin edition had appeared in 1482. But the reasoning powers of the Florentines were too well developed and their imaginations

Study of Herbaceous Flowers,
c. 1481-1483.
Metalpoint, pen and ink,
18.3 x 21 cm.
Galleria dell'Accademia, Venice.

88

too dormant to put much stock into the supernatural. All the naivety, faith and mysticism they possessed were absorbed by the dogma of their irreproachable religious orthodoxy.

Without attempting at present to push the discussion too far, or to anticipate our conclusions, we may allow that in these early years Leonardo dabbled in mysticism, if not in occultism. He was only twenty-one when he adopted the system of writing to which he remained faithful for the rest of his life, that is, the practice of writing from right to left, in the Oriental style. No doubt he wished by this semi-cryptography to put difficulties in the way of anyone who should attempt to rob him of the secrets he had so patiently won.

It is possible that the insatiable spirit of Leonardo, in whom artist and savant competed with such vigour, may have carried him, through pure curiosity, to the fountainhead of mysticism (that is, to the East) for the solution of the doubts by which he was haunted.

In establishing himself in Milan, Leonardo became part of a superstitious society, if ever there was one. Lodovico Sforza supported an army of astrologers, whom he consulted upon every resolution of any importance. We may easily believe that the newcomer became friendly enough with a whole crowd of superstitious Milanese. The reader has already been introduced to the mysterious Jacopo Andrea and to the quasi fellow-countryman of Leonardo, Fra Luca Pacioli, professor of mathematics and a fervent disciple of Pythagoras.

In view of Leonardo's horror of all kinds of publicity, it is easy to believe that he preferred to teach *viva voce*, like the philosophers of antiquity. This, moreover, will explain how, although he never published a line of his manuscripts, a certain number of his discoveries came to the knowledge of Cardan and other intellectuals of the time.

On his return to Florence, Leonardo surrounded himself with two pupils who, at least, devoted themselves to all sorts of mystic speculations. One of these was the eminent sculptor, Rustici, who endowed the Baptistery of his native city with a superb group and finished his days in France, at the court of Henry II. This master wasted his life and fortune on experiments in the freezing of mercury. He had for assistant and accomplice one Raffaello Baglioni.

Once again we find Leonardo in relation with one of those inquisitive and mystery-loving spirits in which Italy was so rich. After telling us that Giuliano de' Medici, the brother of Leo X, attached the painter to himself, Vasari hastens to add that the prince was an ardent student of philosophy and especially of alchemy.

Compromising friendships like this created arguments with d'Annunzio and his co-believers. No one enjoyed the mystification of his circle more than he did. Sometimes he would arrange, in some room adjoining that in which his friends were assembled, the lower section of a sheep's bowel, carefully cleaned and stripped of fat. This, with the help of a forge bellows, he would blow up to such a size that his visitors were driven into a corner, or even out of the house altogether. The moral extracted by Leonardo from such an experiment gives it some right to remembrance, for he compared virtue to one of these transparent bowels, which began by being so small and then became so vast! On another occasion, during his journey to Rome, he modelled animals in wax, hollow and so light that when blown into they would float away through the air. After his arrival on the banks of the Tiber and installation by Leo X in the Vatican, he amused himself by concocting a sort of demon lizard, giving it huge eyes, a beard, horns and wings, to which an injection of quicksilver gave a trembling movement. This remarkable beast he used to carry about in a box, bringing it out to frighten his friends. He also used to terrify his guests by making the outline of a skeleton appear in the shadowed part of a room.

In any other country but Italy, he would have run the risk of the stake, as a sorcerer or magician, but such an idea was foreign to the Holy Inquisition. Leonardo, of course, took precautions to guard against the theft of his discoveries and so was not over-anxious to communicate the fruits of his own toil. Only a foolish inventor would do otherwise. Take the terms esoteric and hermetic in their common meaning, as characterizing the initiation into certain practices that are only handed down through a very small number of pupils and under the seal of secrecy. It is then clear that the whole practice of the founder of the Milanese Academy was inconsistent with any approval of methods so contrary to the scientific spirit.

Study of Anemones in Flower,
c. 1506-1508.
Pen and ink on black chalk,
8.5 x 14 cm.
Royal Library, Windsor Castle.

No doubt, as the Marchese d'Adda has told us, he manipulated crucibles and alembics, distilled perfumes and purified oils, prepared pigments, varnishes and acids, composed mixtures for fireworks or fumes – he never failed to explore the unknown.

In denying the value of chiromancy, he has even shown himself more clear-sighted than Aristotle. In short, it is safe to assert that views so deep and broad have never been allied with such powers of minute observation.

No savant of his time pronounced himself so categorically as Leonardo against all false doctrine. His "magic" consisted in digging more deeply and with more independence than anyone else had shown, into the mysteries of Nature. His curiosity drew him, no doubt, towards the sciences which were called occult, but the incomparable rectitude of his judgment kept him from being in any way their dupe. He loved to play with fire, but he took good care that his fingers remained intact.

Leonardo anticipated Copernicus in propounding the theory of the earth's movement. This we know from the following passage, first brought to light by Venturi:

"Of a weight descending through the air, the entire revolution of the elements of the movement of circumvolution takes place in twenty-four hours. The moving object descending from the highest part of the fiery sphere, will move straight towards the earth, as all the elements are in a continual motion of circumvolution round the centre of the globe. It can be proved. Let b be the falling weight, moving from a in order to descend to m, the centre of the world; I say that such a weight, even while it makes a descent curved in the fashion of a helical line, never deviates from its rectilinear descent under which (it) advances continually between the place it left and the centre of the world; because it left point a and has descended to b. During the time it took in descending to b, it has been carried to d, the position of a has been changed to c and so the moving body finds itself in the right line which extends between c and the centre of the world m. If the moving body descends from d to f, c, principle of the movement, moves in the same time from c to f, [e] and if f descends to h, it turns itself at g and so in twenty-four hours the moving body descends to the earth (at a point) under that from which it started."

In the margin, Leonardo has written: "If the moving body descends from the highest part of the elements to the lowest in twenty-four hours, its movement is composed of straight lines and curves. I say straight, because it never deviates from the very short line which extends between the place from which it started in the centre of the elements and it will stop at the lowest extremity of such a straight line, which will always be found, with respect to the zenith, under the point from which the moving body separated itself. And this movement is curved in itself with all parts of the line. Hence it is that a stone cast from a tower does not strike against the side of the tower before it reaches the ground."

Elsewhere, Leonardo declares in so many words that the sun does not move: *"il sole non si move."*

Mechanics owe a crowd of other discoveries and inventions to Leonardo. It is also said that he was the first in modern times to turn his attention to the centres of gravity of solid bodies, though he had but imperfectly solved the problem of the fall of weights.

We shall look in vain for the name of Leonardo in the works of writers who have related the genesis of the steam engine.

The museum at Valenciennes possesses a drawing by Leonardo that represents a spit turned by steam or, more exactly, by the air rarefied by the heat of the fire.

As a practical mechanic Leonardo was gifted with extraordinary powers. He played with marvellous facility and adaptability with such matters as beams, supports, cranes and escapements. At a time when the use of iron was still very restricted, he was lavish with his cogwheels, his pulleys, in fact with all those refinements, which, in our century, have led to the substitution of machine labor for that of men.

Among instruments invented by his untiring brain we hear of an ingenious pedometer, of several machines for laminating iron, for making cylinders, files, saws and screws for shaving cloth, for winding, for planning, a mechanical press, a gold beater's hammer, a machine for digging ditches and one for tilling the soil with the help of the wind, more than one sounding apparatus, paddle-wheels for boats and lamps with double currents of air.

Asses and an Ox,, c. 1478-1480.
Black chalk, pen and ink
16.7 x 17.7 cm.
Royal Library, Windsor Castle.

Aerial navigation gave him many a sleepless night.

If we brought together all the separate fragments Leonardo wrote on these subjects, fragments numbered in thousands, we should have a vast treatise on physics; he touched on gravity, equilibrium, compressibility, elasticity, the action of heat, fusion, dilatation, on the radiation of heat, optics and acoustics, magnetism, lavishing on each the most striking definitions and the most luminous generalizations. He anticipated Pascal in noting that any liquid in communicating vessels, however different in form those vessels might be, remained at the same level in each (*Codex Atlanticus,* fol. 314). This was the principle of the hydraulic press invented in 1653. He forestalled Chevreul in laying down with perfect clarity the laws governing complementary colours, showing, for instance, that red gained in intensity when placed in juxtaposition with green.

Leonardo was the first to note that the sun's light is more brilliant on the tops of mountains than at their bases. He attributes the difference to the fact that the layer of air between the summit of a mountain and the sun is not as thick as that between the sun and its base. This observation – with which Deluc has been wrongly credited – has been confirmed by Saussure and Humboldt.

He had a glimpse of the telescope and he wrote: "*Fa ochiali da vedere la luna grande.*" Nevertheless, as I have said on a previous page, to assert and to prove are two different things and it is a long way from a simple wish to realization.

Optics excited his interest more than any other branch of physics; he studied it in every manner possible. The study he devoted to the "camera obscura" shows how long it takes common humanity to accept the notion of the most elementary phenomena. Aristotle had already noticed that if a square hole were cut in a window shutter, the beam of light was thrown through it by the sun nevertheless he described a circle on the wall; absorbed by the anomaly, he omits to push his investigations into its cause. Eighteen centuries would pass before anything more would be discovered. Leonardo says that if you place yourself in a hermetically closed room, facing a building, landscape, or any other object directly lighted by the sun and then cut a small circular hole in the shutter, images of the objects outside will be thrown on any surface facing the hole and will be reversed.

The theory of complementary colours, so indissolubly connected with the name of Chevreul, is found in the *Trattato della Pittura.* "If you wish that the neighbourhood of one colour should

Study of a Bear, c. 1480.
Metalpoint, 10.3 x 13.4 cm.
The Metropolitan Museum of
Art, New York.

lend charm to the colour near it, observe what happens when the sun's rays form the rainbow, or iris; the colours are begotten by the movement of the rain, for each drop changes, in tailing, into each of the colours of this rainbow, as will be proved in its proper place." A few lines further on Leonardo will describe the juxtaposition of green and red.

He has left few notes on the conduct of the loadstone, but those notes show a wonderful grasp of his subject. He established the fact that, given an equality of weight, the loadstone and iron attract each other in the same proportion.

With chemistry he had only a passing attraction; it interested him chiefly because of its connection with the preparation of pigments.

He had, nevertheless, a good grasp on the conditions of combustion. "Fire," he says, "continually destroys the air by which it is nourished. It would create a vacuum if more air did not rush in to fill the space. When air is not in a proper condition to receive flame, neither flame nor any animal, terrestrial or aerial, can live in it. No animal can live where a flame cannot live."

Does not this give a complete definition of the part played by oxygen and that two and a half centuries before Lavoisier made his immortal discoveries? Nothing is wanting but the name of the gas and the idea of employing scales to weigh the products of calcinations, before and after. (Berthelot, however, reminds me that similar ideas are to be found in the works of Aristotle and Cicero.)

In the domain of natural science, Leonardo was a student of anatomy, botany and geology.

Leonardo was the first to propose the division of animals into two broad classes: those which have their skeletons inside them and those which have it outside, a division which would correspond roughly with the two classes of vertebrates and invertebrates as fixed by Lamarck and generally adopted until superseded by the evolutionary theories of our own time.

Leonardo discovered the circulation of blood, but he failed to explain its mechanism. "The heart," he says, "is a muscle of great strength, much stronger, than the other muscles... The blood which returns when the heart opens again is not the same as that which closes the valves."

We must remember, he adds, that Leonardo consecrates numerous chapters in the *Trattato della Pittura* to the description of the muscles of the body, of the joints of the limbs, of "the sinews and tendons which gather themselves up when a specific muscle swells in order to produce a specific action."

In what he says about growth, we may note the interesting remark that at the age of two years people have reached one half of what is to be their final height. According to my learned colleague, Edmond Perrier, this rule is fairly exact.

It is in geology, however, that Leonardo claims the largest tribute of admiration by the originality of his views and the boldness of his conjectures. No one before him had penetrated so deeply into the mysterious cataclysms of our globe. His hypotheses, veritable strokes of genius as they are, are directly related to those of Lyell and Darwin. He does not even begin to discuss the Biblical tradition as to the date of creation; his estimates date earlier by hundreds and thousands of centuries. He is not embarrassed by the most appalling ideas of distance. After assigning to the accumulations formed by the River Po a duration of 200,000 years, he prophesizes that all the rivers that now fall into the Mediterranean will end by being tributaries of the Nile and that the latter will have its mouth at the Straits of Gibraltar, just as the rivers which once fell into the gulf of the Po are now tributaries of the Po itself.

Long before Bernard Palissy, who has been called a leader in all these studies, had fixed his attention upon the shells found upon the tops of mountains. He shows that their presence at such a situation had nothing to do with any universal flood and he sets out the bases of his belief with a rare logical incisiveness.

These are his arguments: these shells were not deposited by the Great Flood, as is proven by the fact that they are all found at one level, while the summits of many mountains rise above that level; otherwise, they ought to appear at the summits of these mountains and not at a short distance from their bases. To suppose that these molluscs, accustomed to life at the edge of the sea had come to these places during the Flood, we would have to believe that these very slow-moving animals had made their way from the borders of the Adriatic to

Montferrat in Lombardy, a distance of 250 miles (thousands of cubits), during the forty days of rain which fell during the deluge. To those who assert that they were carried by the waves, Leonardo answers that shellfish, having regard to their weight could only travel at the bottom of the sea. "If you will not allow this," adds the implacable logician, "confess at least that they must have been left on the tops of the highest mountains or in lakes at their bases such as those of Como, Fiesole, Perugia and the Lago Maggiore."

Leonardo defended himself to Cuvier by showing that the level of the seabed is continually rising, sometimes suddenly and rapidly, sometimes by slow accumulations of all kinds of "debris". Mountains, according to him, are both made and destroyed by rivers. Their summits may have been the beds of rivers or seas; but these, driven to retire by the slow corrosion of the mountain bases, have had to form other beds.

With his more abstract studies, Leonardo mingled with practical applications and inventions, often of the humblest kind, such as vehicles, locks for canals, reduction-compasses with movable centres, instruments and machines of many kinds for drawing wire and twisting ropes.

Leonardo, unlike most of his successors, laid down principles at the same time as he contrived applications. Occasionally he even had the chance of seeing his contrivances at work. He thus united in his own person three individuals, the theorist, the mechanical inventor and the engineer, who are almost invariably distinct, as Berthelot has so well explained in his work on Denis Papin.

He was also distinguished as a military engineer. Indeed, if we can judge from his letter to Lodovico Sforza, it was in that department that he himself believed that he chiefly excelled.

Here, as in artistic matters, he took from the Greeks and Romans a great deal more than is usually supposed. His hero was Archimedes, whose biography he may have read in Plutarch's *Lives*. Like the famous Syracusan, he flattered himself because he could rout the enemy by the aid of his miraculous machines. However, while Archimedes long held the Roman armies in check with inventions, which, after all, he only put forward as more or less playful experiments in geometry, Leonardo never, as far as we know, succeeded in applying any of his own redoubtable contrivances of which he speaks.

A long series of drawings acquaints us with the more or less chimerical contrivances of da Vinci. Sometimes he shows us horses armed with lances, at others chariots with hooks and

Allegory of the State of Milan,
c. 1485-1487.
Pen and ink, 20.6 x 28.3 cm.
Christ Church, Oxford.

scythes upon their wheels. Here we see a sort of flying defence, a kind of screen, intended to shelter archers (Valton's collection and others), there, new sorts of battering rams, ballistas and catapults.

He forewarned the inventors of the twentieth century suggesting breech-loading guns and mitrailleuses with many barrels, fixed or movable *(Codex Atlanticus)*. According to the information I have received from Henry de Geymüller, certain engines of this nature are to be found in many collections of arms, in Venice among other places.

No doubt his advice on the construction of flying bridges also contains many valuable suggestions.

In the matter of hydraulics, Leonardo passed for the inventor of many practical innovations and also a vast number of small projects, the credit for which has been taken from him in view of recent research, especially information concerning Beltrami.

Let's now turn to Leonardo's canals. Vasari declares that Leonardo, while still a youth, elaborated a scheme for a navigable canal between Florence and Pisa. He did not propose to embank and dredge the Arno, as Viviani did later on, but to dig a separate

canal that would start from the Arno and cross the districts of Prato, Pistoia, Serravalle and the lake of Sesto. Leonardo discussed the methods of supplying the canal with water, the cost of construction and the mode of dealing with the streams that cross it *(Codex Atlanticus,* f. 45-92).

To Milan, cut off both from the great lakes and the main rivers of northern Italy, the question of inland navigation was always vital. So the public gratitude to Leonardo, which credits him with the whole of these great works of canalisation, is easily understood.

Self-centred as he was, Leonardo was:

"a sower of ideas who would not to see the harvest. His writings are like those grains of wheat that, though lying for ages inert in tombs, germinate as soon as they are restored to the conditions required for development. They only came out into the light long after his death. A profound savant and an incomparable creator, he is the only man in the history of our race who has at once penetrated into the most secret hiding places of truth and evoked visions of the most radiant beauty, who has united the science of Aristotle with the art of Phidias".

Allegory on the Fidelity of a Lizard, 1496.
Pen and brown ink,
20.2 x 13.3 cm.
The Metropolitan Museum of Art,
New York.

Fight between a Dragon and a Lion, Florence.

IV. THE DOWNFALL OF LODOVICO IL MORO AND THE CONSEQUENCES

L odovico's fall was the greatest misfortune that could have happened to Leonardo. He then needed to, just as old age was closing in upon him, find another patron, just like the beginning of his career, a career that had been more fruitful in the masterpieces and the admiration they had won than in tangible reward. It also exposed him to his fear of the dispersal and frittering away of his admirable powers.

When Louis XII made his triumphal entry into Milan on 6 October 1499, accompanied by Cæsar Borgia and a bevy of great lords, the wonders wrought by Leonardo's brush and chisel were among the first objects to fix his attention. He had such ecstatic admiration for the *Last Supper* that for a moment he dreamt of carrying it off to France along with the wall on which it was painted. He was no less fascinated by the equestrian statue of Francesco Sforza.

Yet, for some reason, Louis XII, who left Milan and returned to France on November 7 1499, allowed several years to elapse before he finally attached the author of these masterpieces to his own service.

Leonardo went to Mantua, to the Marchesa Isabella d'Este.

His departure from Milan took place somewhere during the latter months of the year 1499, shortly after the occurrence of the disasters in il Moro.

The name of the Marchesa Isabella d'Este was heard, the wife of Giovanni Francesco di Gonzaga and sister-in-law of Lodovico Sforza, it calls up the figure of the most accomplished woman of the Italian Renaissance. She was full of boundless eagerness for intellectual pleasures and she had an exquisite taste combined with the highest moral virtues. Irreproachable as a wife, wise and tender as a mother, a patriot during that critical time when patriotism suffered so utter an eclipse – (it was she, who, when hearing of the gallant resistance of the city of Faënza, besieged by Cæsar Borgia, exclaimed: "They have saved the honour of Italy!") – she counted all the men who shed the most glory on the Renaissance among her clients, her friends and her admirers.

Notwithstanding her own frequent journeys to Milan, Isabella does not appear to have entered into personal contact with the painter before Leonardo's visit in 1499. At the most she seems to have written to Cecilia Gallerani, in 1498, to beg her to send da Vinci's portrait of herself.

It was certainly during his visit to Mantua that Leonardo painted this portrait.

Leonardo's departure did not interrupt his relationship with the learned and witty Isabella. Their friendship was limited to an exchange of correspondence. Leonardo's nature was such that the work undertaken by him for his various patrons rarely passed beyond purely platonic affiliation.

Leonardo, as Tovaglia had predicted, won the laggard's prize at last and the Marchesa, though disheartened, put away her hopes. From 1506 onwards, no trace of any correspondence between her and the all too unpunctual Florentine is to be found.

The period between 1501 and 1514 is the period that gave birth to the greater number of pictures painted by Leonardo, then over fifty years of age. Having no more orders for monumental works (except for the *Battle of Anghiari*), he turned his attention to more modest productions; a fortunate necessity to which we owe the *Saint Anne*, the *Mona Lisa*, and *St John the Baptist*.

During this epoch, Leonardo solved the secret of simultaneously working on his engineering labours and his work as a painter and moved perpetually between Florence and the towns of Umbria and the Romagna.

The last period of Leonardo's career, the evening of his splendid life, opens with regrettable determination, a capitulation of his conscience: disheartened, the master entered the service of Cæsar Borgia, as his military engineer.

Portrait of a Lady (The Beautiful Ferronniere), 1495-1499.
Oil on wood panel, 63 x 45 cm.
Musée du Louvre, Paris.

Portrait of Isabella d'Este, 1500.
Black chalk with touches of red chalk in hair and skin and highlights in yellow pastel in the dress, 61 x 46 cm.
Musée du Louvre, Paris.

Head of Dishevelled Young Girl (La Scapiliata), 1500.
Burnt umber and green umber and highlights of white on wood panel, 24.7 x 21 cm.
Galleria Nazionale, Parma.

The fate that weighed on the Italy of the Renaissance ordained that its three greatest artists should serve as her victims and her executioners in turn. Even as Leonardo was forced to wield his brush in honour of Lodovico il Moro and Louis XII, or to serve the Dictator of the Romagna – so Raphael, after having celebrated the glories of his rightful sovereign, the Duke of Urbino, was fain to make up his mind to work for that sovereign's despoiler, Lorenzo de' Medici.

In Leonardo's case, one would willingly discover that side by side in the thinker and the moralist was a generous heart, full of passionate interest in all the struggles that marked his period. But this would be a delusion. As Séailles has most truly pointed out, he looked at political phenomena like a Spinoza: "*sub specie æterni,*" from the eternal point of view. The evil wrought by others interested him less than the good he could do himself. Politics and social organization, therefore, offered no attraction to the solitary speculator who was accustomed to hover far above the level of the questions of the day.

The foregoing statement was indispensable for the definition of the point of view from which we must judge a nature as rich as it was vacillating.

After his visit to Venice in March 1500, Leonardo returned like the prodigal son to his native city. He took up his residence for six months in the house of his young disciple, the sculptor Giovanni Francesco Rustici. He had saved money during his stay in Milan proven by the fact that he deposited 600 florins at the Hospice of "Santa Maria Nuova" in the month of January 1500. On various occasions, between 24 April 1500 and 20 May 1506, he drew out 450 florins of this sum.

Leonardo returned to Florence famous and admired. Did his country realize, at last, that in the case of a man of such genius, the current rate of production must be put aside; that perfection so great could only be attained by meticulous and infinite toil?

No man was ever less prone to improvisation; in those days of easy production, da Vinci represented the very extreme of scrupulous care. He alone might, by his sole example, have checked the already visible decline of the Florentine school. The respect for nature and worship of form that he professed was the remedy – and the only efficacious one – for a degeneration of which all too many symptoms were apparent.

The Gonfaloniere Pietro Soderini was anxious to do something for the sorely-tried artist.

For a moment there was a question of confiding the famous block of marble, out of which Michelangelo ultimately sculptured the David, to Leonardo's chisel (Michelangelo was given this commission in accordance with deliberations held on July 2 and August 16 1501), but the expiration of Soderini's period of power – he was not appointed Gonfaloniere for life, until September 22 1502 – paralyzed the great official's well meant efforts.

Meanwhile, Leonardo painted his *Saint Anne*. In the month of April 1501, he began working upon it eagerly, but he soon put it aside half finished as he did with so many other pictures. In the following September, he was travelling about as the military engineer to Cæsar Borgia.

This was the first occasion, most likely, where Leonardo da Vinci was permitted to realize a long-cherished dream: the ability to give practical evidence of his skill in the art of war. For a long time this had been his supreme ambition.

Saint Anne

Leonardo laid the first touches on one his masterpiece, the *Saint Anne*, in the meantime.

Vasari, having heard that the Servites had commissioned Filippino Lippi to paint the picture for the high altar of the 'Nunziata', expressed his desire to receive an order for some similar work. With which Filippino, like the kindly and courteous man he was, made the commission for him. The brothers, to ensure Leonardo every comfort, received him in their house, entertaining both him and his following (that following which stood him in the stead of family). At last, he produced a sketch, with the Madonna, St Anne and the Christ. Not only did this work, Vasari adds that it "filled all the artists with admiration, but on its completion, a continuous procession of men and women, of old men and youths, who hastened to

Study for the Christ Child,
1501-1510.
Red chalk with white highlights
on paper, 28.5 x 19.8 cm.
Galleria dell'Accademia, Venice.

102

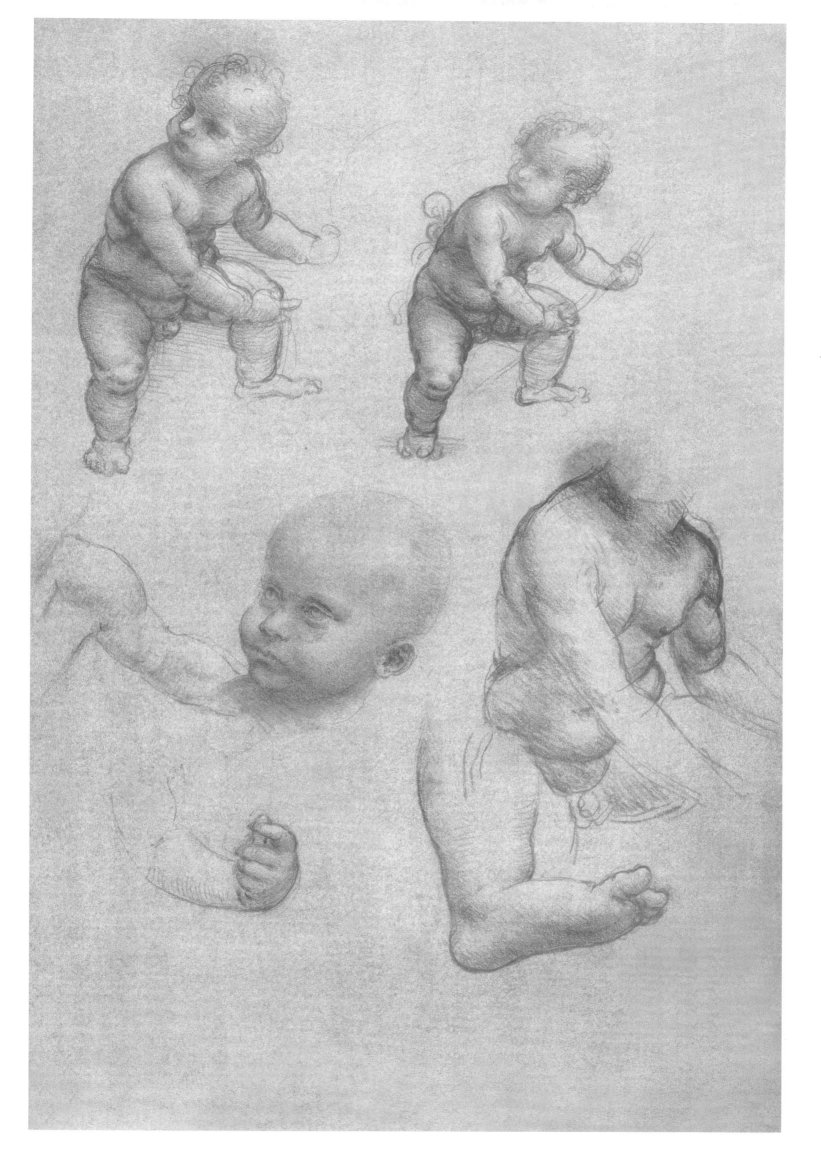

admire the masterpiece, filled the chamber in which it was exhibited for two whole days. The whole town was in frenzy as if it were a holiday.

"The face of the Virgin shows all that simplicity, beauty and grace which characterize the Mother of Christ along with her modesty and humility, mixed with joy at the sight of the beautiful Child she holds so lovingly on her lap. Her eyes, too, rest kindly on little St John, playing with his lamb, while the smile of St Anne expresses her deep joy at beholding the association of her terrestrial descendants with celestial glory— a kind of expression that, as is well known, was specially suited to Leonardo's talent. This sketch, as will be shortly shown, was carried off to France. Leonardo having relinquished the undertaking, the brothers once more confided it to Filippino, but with death overtaking him, he was not able to accomplish it. Later on: "Leonardo went to France for the King, who possessed some of his works and showed him great affection and expressed his desire to see the sketch of *Saint Anne* carried out in color; but he, as was his wont, put him off, for a long time, with words."

The history of this masterpiece is exceedingly obscure. For many years, the work that is now preserved in the Royal Academy in London was thought to be the Servite sketch, but this differs in several points from Vasari's description. Little St John the Baptist is not playing with a lamb; he is advancing towards the Holy Child as though he is making Him homage and the Child's right hand is raised to bless him. Further, note that St Anne points her finger heavenward, a gesture that would not have escaped Vasari's notice. The London sketch is most certainly only the very earliest conception of the composition. It may be that it was produced at a different period and intended for another picture. This would explain why only one artist, Bernardino Luini, thought of copying it (his picture is now preserved in the Ambrosiana at Milan), whereas the final sketch gave birth to a score of copies or imitations.

Personally, I am inclined to believe that the painting in the Louvre is the sketch executed for the Servites and that there are several inaccuracies in the description of it by Vasari. One thing is for certain: that all the sixteenth-century writers – including Paolo Giovio and other anonymous authors – that speak of a *Saint Anne* purchased by Francis I. Furthermore, when the Cardinal Louis d'Aragon paid a visit to Leonardo at the Chateau de Cloux in 1516, the artist showed him a picture of the "*Madonna e del figliolo che stan posti in gremmo di Sancta Anna.*" This, evidently, is the *Saint Anne* in the Louvre.

It is true that the Louvre picture does differ in some aspects from the description by Vasari, but that description was very likely founded on hearsay. Vasari never went to Florence until 1528 and thus had no opportunity to study the picture with his own eyes and, as we shall shortly learn, it had left Italy long before that date. I will limit myself to the indication of a few of the divergences. The biographer mentions, among the different figures in the sacred idyll, the infant St John the Baptist. Now there is no figure of St John in the Louvre picture. He also tells us that the Child Jesus is seated on His Mother's lap. In the Louvre picture, the Child is sitting on the ground and just about to bestride the lamb. Fortunately, a valuable document was discovered in the archives from Mantua by Armand Baschet and published by Charles Yriarte cast a flood of light upon this matter.

This letter removes all doubt as to the identity of the composition selected for the picture in the Louvre with that produced by Leonardo in 1501. Leonardo has represented the Infant Christ escaping from His Mother's arms, to lay hands on a lamb. The Virgin rises, almost from her mother's lap to separate the Child from the lamb and that St Anne seems disposed to hold her daughter back. These features are applicable in every characteristic to the sketch in the Louvre, except that, in the latter, St Anne, with one hand on her hip, quietly watches her grandson's play instead of making any effort to prevent her daughter from restraining him. None of these features, on the other hand, are applicable to the Royal Academy sketch – the lamb is entirely absent (its place is supplanted by the figure of the infant St John the Baptist). The scene, therefore, is quite different in both aspect and significance to that described by Fra Pietro da Nuvolaria, who further gives us the date at which the composition was definitely decided upon in Leonardo's mind– April 1501.

Saint Anne, the Madonna and the Child with the Infant Saint John the Baptist, 1499-1500. Sketch, 141.5 x 104.6 cm. The National Gallery, London.

When Leonardo returned to Milan to reside there, he naturally took his drawing with him. This explains the frequent reproduction of his charming and wonderfully harmonious composition by the painters of northern Italy.

Finally, the sketch followed its author to France.

The idea of representing the Virgin seated on the knee of her mother, St Anne, seemed to have lingered in Leonardo's mind for a long time. Perhaps he hoped the increased strength of the impression would be produced by the contemplation of these two generations of maternity of St Anne for the Virgin and of the Virgin for her Son. However that may have been the idea of this grown woman, already a mother herself, sitting on the lap of her own parent. There is something very-familiar about it, which startles and repels.

Seated on a hillock facing the spectator with her figure thrown back, her left arm is leaning on her hip while her two bare feet are planted squarely on the ground as though to steady herself. St Anne, her face shining with happiness, an ineffable smile upon her lips, contemplates the charming group formed by her daughter and her grandson. The Virgin, sitting on her mother's knee is turned to the right and seen in profile only, bends to take up her Son who is playing with a lamb and who – that age knows no pity! – seems to be somewhat tormenting the innocent creature. He has caught hold of one of its ears and thrown one of his legs over its neck, as though desiring to ride upon it. The lamb, though seeming to recognise this as mere caressing sport, gently resists, while the Child, obedient to his mother's voice, turns round as if to say, "But I am not hurting it!"

Any attempt to describe the naturalness, the ease and the charm of this little idyll in written words must be futile indeed. The correctness of the various expressions and the grace of the movements, are as nothing beside the overflowing poetry of the whole picture. In every detail of the work the artist has achieved the wonderful feat of making us forget the skill of the painter in our admiration of the poet, who calls up the most smiling fancies before our eyes. No other artist has based a composition of such apparent lightness and grace on so firm a groundwork of effort and research than Leonardo's work which, consequently, bears more criticism than that of any other master.

Let us not forget that the *Saint Anne* (a sketch only, but what a sketch!) is a complete contrast to the *Virgin of the Rocks*. The extreme of close and careful execution in the latter is balanced by an outburst of fancy and freedom. Leonardo's genius, so radiant in its essence, handles the subject over which it had so long been brooding with consummate ease. Not a trace of effort remains. He has acquired sufficient self-control, sufficient power of abstraction to spare us the sight of the groping and struggles which have led up to his triumph. The work seems to have sprung into existence in a flash and we could not desire or conceive it differently than in any one particular.

The colouring of the *Saint Anne* is clear, tender, sunny, and full of pinks and blues and tender carnations. It foreshadows Luini, Sodoma and Andrea del Sarto. The Virgin wears a reddish dress with sleeves of a shade approaching blue and a bluish mantle. (Positive colours very seldom appear in Leonardo's pictures. Everything, in his case, is relative and subjective. He must have had a foreknowledge of the laws of Daltonism.)

The landscape is light and hazy. Towards the centre on the right stands a clump of trees fuller and leafier than those of the primitive masters, but treated in quite as poetic a style (Leonardo kept his youth so long!). They have the same smooth trunks crowned by sparse, quivering foliage, showing the deep Italian sky in the background. My readers will be glad that I will introduce them to some remarks on Leonardo's landscape art, by my friend Émile Michel, whose opinion carries double weight, as being that both of an artist and an art critic. "Like Mantegna," writes Michel, "Leonardo holds that even as a background to pictures, the mere reproduction of nature does not offer sufficient interest. He searches out strange features and in one and the same work he will bring together, without much air of probability, such curiosities of picturesque scenery as seemingly to him are likely to appeal to the spectator's curiosity.

"The bizarre landscape that stretches behind the *Mona Lisa* certainly does add to the mysterious fascination of that enigmatic figure. The treacherous country, with its jagged peaks,

The Virgin and Child with St Anne, c.1510.
Oil on wood, 168 x 130 cm.
Musée du Louvre, Paris.

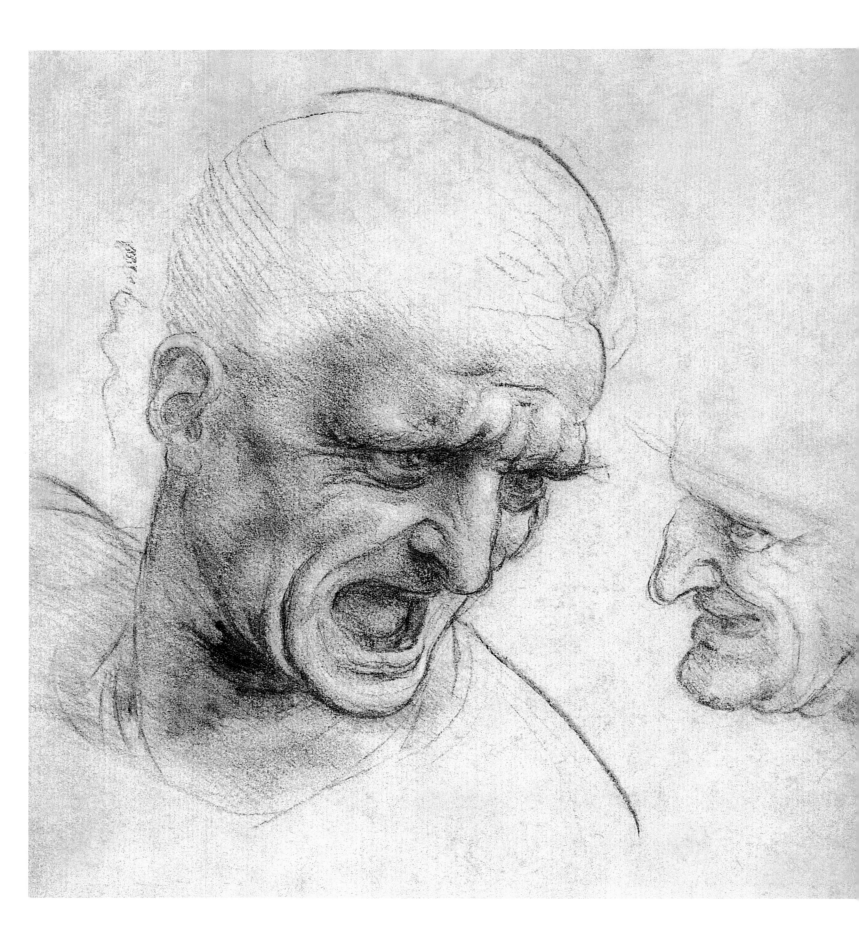

deep waters and winding passes, the leaden sky and the threatening elements, frame the siren's beauty in most expressive fashion.

"The same background of bare bluish peaks appears in the *Saint Anne* overlooking a far more smiling landscape, with waters that spread in rushing cascades amongst the trees and brown patches of earth. The strangeness of Leonardo's backgrounds is increased by the fact that the details of his foregrounds are, as a rule, faithfully taken from nature and reproduced with the scrupulous care and skill in which no artist has ever equalled him. In the *Saint Anne,* every pebble on the ground has been separately and minutely studied while in the *Virgin of the Rocks,* nature is displayed through the fantastic openings of the grotto in which the Virgin is placed, the same mountainous country crowned with sharp bristling peaks while Leonardo has adorned the foreground of his picture with lovingly painted ferns, irises, cyclamens and borage, springing out of the rocky crevices."

Fortunately for Leonardo's fame, the fall of Cæsar Borgia forced him for a time to turn his sole attention to painting.

At the same time, a kind of reaction, on which the great master must be congratulated, drove him, whenever occasion offered, to claim his rights and perform his duties as a Florentine and to interest himself, once more, in matters that concerned his native country.

The circumstances under which his return had taken place did not have fail to strengthen the mutual affection between the painter and his fellow-citizens. Leonardo's glory had gone before him to Florence. He had left the city as a young artist of brilliant promise and he returned as the unquestioned leader of the Italian school. Even masters such as Filippino Lippi hastened to do him favors and to proclaim the most flattering commissions in his honour.

This was the excited condition of men's minds when Leonardo was called by the Florentine Government – then, as we have just seen, presided over by Piero Soderini – to take his share in the decoration of the Palazzo Vecchio.

The Battle of Anghiari

The earliest discussion as to the decoration of the Council Chamber took place during the autumn of 1503. On October 24, the Council commanded the mace-bearer to make over the keys of the Pope's Chamber at Sta Maria Novella to Leonardo's keeping. Here the artist was to prepare his drawing.

"Competition" is a word that has often been used in the course of references to the famous struggle between those two giants of art, Leonardo and Michelangelo. The term, as a matter of fact, is quite inapplicable. "Competition" indicates a preference shown to one party, an elimination of the other.

Nothing of the sort occurs in this case. Each rival receives his own separate order, each treats his separate subject and each has the certain hope of seeing his handiwork shine in perpetual glory in the chief hall of the ancient municipal Palace. The competition, if such there were, is purely platonic. The only object of either artist is to excel the other and win more general applause. It was in this fashion that, some twelve years later, Raphael and Sebastiano del Piombo respectively produced the *Transfiguration* and the *Raising of Lazarus* before the rapt and admiring eyes of Rome.

Contemporary witness, however, is unanimous as to the hostility between Leonardo da Vinci and Michelangelo.

It may be that the opinion expressed by Leonardo on the occasion of the setting up of the *David* gave umbrage to the sculptor. One thing is certain; the younger rival looked askance at the older man's genius. The man who had openly declared Perugino to be a dullard, who had accused Raphael of plagiarism and pronounced the work of one of his best friends, Baccio d'Agnolo puerile, was not disposed to bow his head before an artistic talent which, though less spontaneous and less calculated to impress the vulgar than his own, was

Study for the Battle of Anghiari,
1503-1504.
Red chalk, 22.7 x 18.5 cm.
Szépmüvészeti Muzeum,
Budapest.

in reality far deeper. Vasari tells, in a very confused fashion, a story on this subject, the sense of which, unless I am mistaken, is as follows: Leo X had consulted Leonardo as to the completion of the façade of the church of San Lorenzo at Florence. Hearing this, Michelangelo, who had been commissioned to do the work left Florence with the approval of the Duke, Giuliano de' Medici. Leonardo, in his turn, filled with disgust, made up his mind to travel to France.

Before we actually study Leonardo's composition, let us try to follow up the history of the masterpiece, its vicissitudes and its destruction that was so greatly to be deplored.

For some time already, Leonardo, with the characteristic weakness that so often hampered his work, had been allowing the chemist to get the better of the artist. He had read in Pliny, without thoroughly understanding it, a recipe for some special stucco used by the Roman painters. He had tried it for the first time for his painting in the Pope's Chamber where he was then working. Having placed his picture against the wall, he lit a large charcoal fire in front of it, the heat of which dried and hardened the substance on which he had worked. He endeavoured to employ the same preparation in the Council Hall itself and as a matter of fact, the lower part, which the fire could reach, did dry and harden satisfactorily, and in the upper region, which the heat could not touch because of the distance, the substance remained soft and ran.

This was more than enough to put Leonardo out of heart and, as in the case of the *Adoration of the Magi*, the equestrian statue of Francesco Sforza and many other works, he left his masterpiece alone and began to build fresh castles in the air.

Let us say at once that the sketch on the walls of the Palazzo Vecchio was destined shortly to disappear. On 13 April 1513, the Council of the Florentine Republic gave orders to a carpenter to put up a balustrade to protect the figures painted by Leonardo in the great hall. Then there is silence as to the masterpiece and no one knows how or when it perished.

In this celebrated group Leonardo has rendered, with unspeakable skill all the fury and despair and desperate effort of which the animal frame is capable— its grinding teeth, its yelling throat. We are not standing before a picture; we are in the thick of the fight. Even on the very ground and under the horses' feet, the struggle goes on fiercely. One soldier, brought to his knees, may think only of how to shelter himself behind his buckler from the horse that rears above him; but close beside him two men clinging to each other are engaged in the most deadly strife.

At a first glance the costumes and armour may appear fantastic – the cuirasses with ram's heads in the centre and ram's horns on the shoulders; the helmets adorned with dragons. The turbans and curved swords that look like Turkish scimitars seem more suited to some imaginary army than to real "*condottieri*". Yet a mass of contemporary testimony shows us that the Italians of Leonardo's time did load themselves with such extravagant adornments. It was a caprice characteristic of the men of the Renaissance. Art, they decreed, was to spread its influence even over sciences that seemed to be the negation of all art. The military engineer, the armoured, the very cannon-founder, was looked on as varieties of the artist.

The central group of four horsemen is incomparable in its vigour and fury. Two Florentine centaurs have succeeded in laying hold of the end of the staff of the Milanese standard; one of them has even contrived to break it in half and is grasping the portion to which the banner itself is affixed. While one assailant uses both hands to hold the precious spoil, his comrade brandishes his sword, to keep back a turbaned Milanese who is rushing to the standard-bearer's assistance. The standard-bearer himself is in a very awkward position. His foes, in their efforts to snatch the flag, have brought the pole right behind his back and under his arm; thus he cannot turn to face them and his resistance is reduced to desperate contortions, one hand, clutching the end of the staff, the other thrown behind him. Meanwhile the horses neigh and rear, tearing at each other with their teeth.

The two cartoons of the *Battle of Anghiari* and the *Pisan War* highlight the different temperaments of Leonardo da Vinci and Michelangelo. In Leonardo's work, knowledge, subtleties and distinction, pervade the whole, without weakening the magnificent dash of the composition. Michelangelo's cartoon may be lacking in that science of picturesque grouping,

Fight for the Standard,
16th century.
Black chalk, pen and ink,
42.8 x 57.7 cm.
Musée du Louvre, Paris.

The Battle of Anghiari,
1504-1506.
Oil on wood panel, 85 x 115 cm.
Private collection.

which he never attained at any time, but how eloquent are his athletic forms, how noble his attitudes! How clear, living, dramatic, powerful even to brutality, the whole picture is! The generous passion of liberty, the noble audacity of the old Republic, shone for the last time in this cartoon of Buonarroti's.

Religious and historical art – the *Saint Anne* and the *Battle of Anghiari* – had not so absorbed Leonardo as to leave him no time for less serious work: there is a pendant to these two masterpieces – the most marvellous of all portraits, antique or modern, the glory of the Louvre – the *Mona Lisa*.

Mona Lisa

Poets, novelists, historians and aesthetic students have all had the honour to be the prodigies of execution apparent in the *Mona Lisa* and built up a series of the most ingenious hypotheses as to the character of the original. However, none of them has ever attempted to tear aside the veil that conceals a personality that must have possessed a sovereign attraction, nor searched bygone archives for any enlightenment as to the life and surroundings of Mona Lisa. At first glance, such an enquiry would seem to promise but little interest. The "raison d'être" of the *Mona Lisa* is the genius of Leonardo da Vinci. But for him, the name of this obscure Florentine patrician would never have fallen upon our ears, nor would her image have haunted our imaginations. Nevertheless, I have held it my duty, as an historian, to attack this problem and to add some details, though far from complete, to the biography of Leonardo's heroine.

The Giocondo family was one of the most important in Florence. Mona Lisa's husband, Francesco di Bartolommeo di Zanobi del Giocondo (born 1460, died 1528), filled several important public offices. In 1499 he was one of the twelve "*Buonomini*", in 1512 he was one of the "*Priori*" and was confirmed in the office in 1524.

The Giocondo family loved art and artists. Francesco commissioned Puligo to paint him a *St Francis receiving the Stigmata*. His son caused Antonio di Donnino Mazzieri to paint a *History of the Martyrs* which was intended for the chapel in the Annunziata and contained the family burial ground. Another member of the family, Leonardo, bought a *Madonna* from Andrea del Sarto.

When, in the year 1495, Francesco took to wife Mona Lisa (Mona is an abbreviation of Madonna), he had already, within the space of four years, become a widower two times. He had married Camilla di Mariotto Ruccellai in 1491 and Tommasa di Mariotto Villani in 1493. His third wife was of Neapolitan origin. She belonged to the Gherardini family, possibly a branch of the Florentine stock bearing the same name. Unfortunately, the information I have been able to collect as to this first phase of her existence is limited. The enquiries kindly instituted at my request by Barone, archivist of the Neapolitan state archives, have not bore any fruit. In all probability, the child that died in 1499 and was buried at Santa Maria Novella was the issue of this third marriage and consequently Mona Lisa's daughter.

As for Bartolommeo del Giocondo, to whom we have just referred in connection with a picture by Mazzieri, it is not known whether he was the son of Mona Lisa or of one of Francesco's two former wives. On the theory that Mona Lisa was twenty when she married, she may have been near thirty when her portrait was painted. From that time onward she disappeared into obscurity.

This picture of Mona Lisa has its story; we might almost say its legend. Vasari retells it while Leonardo worked upon it and he was careful to surround his sitter with musicians, singers and buffoons, who kept her in a state of gentle merriment to avoid the look of melancholy apparent in most portraits. And thus, Vasari tells us that "this portrait of Leonardo's wears so delightful a smile that the work looks more divine than human and is considered a most marvellous and life-like thing, even when compared with Nature herself."

There are few studies for the Mona Lisa and – as if the artist had resolved to puzzle us – the primary of these— a red chalk drawing in the Windsor Library of two hands laid one upon the other and another single hand that is strangely unlike the work itself. Its angular forms are

Mona Lisa (La Gioconda) (detail), c. 1503-1506.
Oil on poplar panel, 77 x 53 cm.
Musée du Louvre, Paris.

in complete contrast to the delicate modelling of the actual picture. The fingers are bony and the nails square.

One is tempted, on the other hand, to see a preparatory study for the *Mona Lisa* in the half-length portrait of a nude woman in the Condé Museum at Chantilly. It is quite certain that this painting marks the transition between the *Mona Lisa* and the *Bacchus*.

Any attempt to analyze a marvel that is in every memory and describe a portrait which excels all others in beauty and in fame, must seem superfluous.

My readers are well aware that for centuries Mona Lisa Gioconda has been an indecipherable and fascinating enigma to all the admirers who have crowded about her.

"Never did any other artist (I borrow the words of the delicate writer who conceals his identity under the pseudonym Pierre de Corlay) so reproduce the very essence of woman. There is tenderness and there is coquetry; there is modesty and there is hidden passion; all the mystery of a heart that is itself in reserve; of a brain that reflects; of a person who guards her own individuality and only sheds its radiance on others! Mona Lisa is thirty. Her charms have blossomed out. Her serene beauty, the reflection of her strong cheerful nature, is chaste and tempting at once as well as kind with a touch of malice; proud, but also with a touch of wise condescension to her admirers.

Freely and boldly, sure of herself and of her power, she shows them her forehead, the temples throbbing with eager thought; her eyes, that sparkle with subtle raillery; her delicately curved lips, with their scornful and voluptuous smile; the firm outline of her bosom; the exquisite oval of her face, her patrician hands lying restfully before her. She shows them her whole self, in fact. And yet... she gives them nothing. The source of her thoughts, the deep reason of her smile, the spark that has put that strange light in her eyes are all mysteriously hidden. That is her secret! – the impenetrable secret of her mighty attraction. Time has touched the masterpiece with his magic hand and the violet atmosphere which seems to bathe the great artist's matchless model adds an indescribable fascination to the picture."

Leonardo's heroine has full, almost puffy cheeks and heavy eyelids; on her mouth is that indefinable smile which every art lover knows. The eyebrows and lashes are lacking, because of, no doubt, to some past restoration. Faint traces of them and of the shadow they cast on the cheek, are still discernible through a magnifying glass.

One detail that has been overlooked is that two beautiful painted columns frame the portrait; the current frame hides these, but they are distinctly visible in the (unfinished) engraving by François Gaillard and in several old copies. Their presence is further proof of the artist's worship of the antique.

The chief characteristic of the execution is the care for relief; for example, the hands with their matchless modelling are quite deceptive. They would almost be classified as a deliberate essay in illusion, if the touch were less broad and flexible.

What knowledge, what calculation is involved! None but the mightiest genius, such as Phidias or Leonardo could have evolved such a perfect synthesis from vast meditations!

The rocky landscape is as full of detail as those of Mantegna. It shows us, besides its dolomite rocks, a winding road, a bridge and many other things. Nothing could be further removed from the ample and harmonious landscapes of the Umbrian school.

With regard to this landscape and those of Leonardo in general, Emile Michel, whose own reproductions of the most picturesque scenes are as skilful as his written comments on the work of former landscapists, writes:

"In a letter addressed by Rumohr to Alexander von Humboldt, he declaims against the idea put forward by the author of *Kosmos* to the effect that the steep mountains which appear in the pictures by the early masters were a memory of the dolomite cones to be seen on certain Italian slopes of the Alps. He considers them as being more probably conventional imitations of antique bas-reliefs, or even perhaps fanciful forms. I believe that Humboldt and Rumohr are

Mona Lisa (La Gioconda),
c. 1503-1506.
Oil on poplar panel, 77 x 53 cm.
Musée du Louvre, Paris.

both right; that the Primitives and after them Mantegna and Leonardo, may have found the elements of their picturesque backgrounds in nature, but that they have exaggerated the details according to their own fancy, after a fashion which may be remarked in early Flemish landscape art, where also the Primitives multiplied detail, spreading out wide panoramas, accumulating buildings and mountains and watercourses. In Leonardo's case," adds Michel; "the ground is treated as by Mantegna, cut up, in the foreground, in regular strata, hewn into sharp ridges, as in the works of the Primitives. The vegetation, on the other hand, is carefully studied. The artist's manuscripts prove how much botany occupied his attention."

Posterity has lavished expressions of admiration, almost of adoration, on the masterpiece in the Salon Carré. But do any one of these approaches, either in eloquence or scope, analyse of the picture left to us by the earliest of all Leonardo's biographers, Giorgio Vasari?

"He who would know," he writes, "to what point nature may be imitated, can easily discover it by considering this head, in which Leonardo has represented the smallest details with an extreme subtlety. The eyes have the light and moisture seen in a living person: they are circled with reddish and leaden shadows of perfect truthfulness; the lashes fringing them are painted with excessive delicacy. The eyebrows, the way in which they spring from the flesh, their varying thickness, the manner in which they curve according to the pores of the skin, could not have been rendered in a more natural fashion. The mouth, its opening, the corners, where the vermilion of the lips fades into the flesh of the cheeks – this is no painting, it is real flesh. An attentive observer might almost see the artery throb in the hollow of the throat; it must be acknowledged that the execution of this figure is calculated to make the most skilful artist in the world draw back at the idea of attempting to imitate it."

Vasari adds that after four years of assiduous labor, Leonardo left his work unfinished. What must have been the perfection of the ideal that floated in the master's brain, if he held such a finished masterpiece to be incomplete? We know the portrait in the Louvre has passed through some cruel experiences. What must have been the original beauty of the incomparable work, which, even defaced as it is now, still shines with so much radiance?

Leonardo, in his *Trattato della Pittura*, has treated at length of the relative superiority of painting over poetry. Was he not thinking of the *Mona Lisa* when he penned those memorable lines: "What poet, O lover, can make thine idol live before thine eyes as faithfully as does the painter?" Can any poem in the world, indeed, contend for mastery with such a picture?

It is hardly probable that the portrait of *Mona Lisa* was the female portrait ordered by Giuliano de' Medici and seen in Leonardo's studio by the Cardinal d'Aragon in 1516. However that may have been, it is certain that this artistic gem was acquired by Francis I, at the price of 4000 gold crowns. *Mona Lisa was* one of the glories of the Palace of Fontainebleau until after the reign of Louis XIV.

Man has more cruelly treated the masterpiece than time has. Over-zealous conservators have ruined it in their desire to ensure its preservation. As early as 1625, the Commendatore del Pozzo noticed the ravages made by varnish on the dress.

Durand-Greville's research has elicited the fact that before time and varnish together had done their work, the sky of the picture was of a pale delicate blue, the face dazzlingly clear and fresh, every eyelash carefully studied and the eyes at once brilliant and liquid.

Leonardo's relations with the Giocondo family were not limited – according to the anonymous biography published by Milanesi – to his portrait of Mona Lisa. The artist appears to have also painted a portrait of Piero Francesco del Giocondo. But may not this be simply a confusion of names? The same anonymous pen informs us, as does Vasari, that while at Florence, Leonardo painted a portrait of Ginevra Benci, daughter or wife of Amerigo Benci.

Of late years, a learned critic of Tuscan art, Ridolfi, has questioned Vasari's statement, upon the following grounds. Ginevra di Amerigo Benci was born in 1457; she married Luigi di Bernardo Niccolini in 1473 and died the same year. Leonardo, then, must have painted

Study for the Head of the Virgin, 1508-1512.

Soft chalk, 20.3 x 15.6 cm.

The Metropolitan Museum of Art, New York.

Drapery Study for the Madonna,
c. 1510. Black chalk, brush and
brown wash, 23 x 24.5 cm.
Musée du Louvre, Paris.

120

her picture before he went to Milan and not after his return to Florence. He painted her, in fact, as Vasari asserts, while she was still a child, *"quando era una fanciulla, e bellissima."* Two other young girls of the family did, it is true, bear the same name, Ginevra di Bartolommeo di Giovanni d'Amerigo Benci, who was two years old in 1480 and Ginevra di Donato d'Amerigo Benci, who was three years old at the same period.

Rosini, the historian of Italian painting, quoted, in support of Vasari, a portrait in his own possession that he asserted to be Leonardo's original portrait. However, this very mediocre work, which was bequeathed to the National Museum at Florence by Carrand, shows no traces of Leonardo's hand.

These portraits lead me, by a natural transition, to consider Leonardo's ideal of female beauty and the place occupied by woman in his life and work. I see a long and fascinating array, from the *Three Dancing Girls,* or *Bacchantes,* one of the young master's earliest drawings, down to the *Mona Lisa*

There is no recognized and authentic female portrait executed by Leonardo in his youth. All we have are a few drawings and two or three sacred pictures (the authenticity of only one, the *Virgin of the Rocks*), whereby we may guess at the type that then hovered before the eyes of the young beginner.

There is something very vague about the faces. We will find it hard to discover any of what I weould call a well-assimilated and well-matured type. Both the form of the faces and their expressions are still somewhat uncertain. The artist's hand had not yet the full command of his instruments.

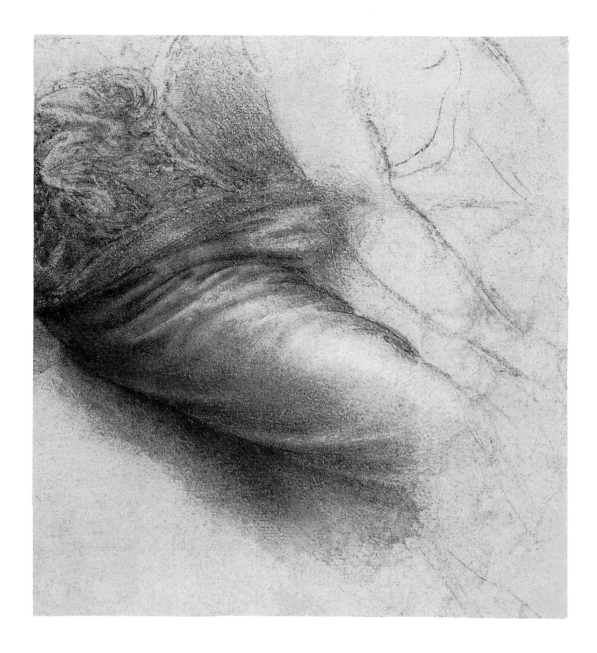

There is more decision in the fine drawing of the Uffizi Gallery: a young woman with long unattached hair downcast eyes and lips straight rather than curved, facing the spectator.

In this drawing, as in the *Virgin of the Rocks*, Leonardo shows his preference for low and somewhat square chins. The same peculiarity is observable in the work of Bernardino Luini. At a later period, the artist is careful to round his chins so as to secure the most perfect oval possible and shows a preference for high and rounded chins. This inclination, already evident in his study for the *Madonna Litta* of the Hermitage, is still more clearly shown in the study of a woman's head, on green paper, preserved in the Uffizi Museum, which I think may be connected with the *Saint Anne*.

Dreamy eyes, a somewhat strongly marked nose, a melancholy mouth, a shade of gentleness, kindness, almost of weakness, over every feature, characterize a profile study in the Louvre, wonderfully rich and easy in handling. This is the drawing above mentioned for the *Madonna Litta*.

As a pendant to this somewhat sickly physiognomy, we have the face of a young girl, of a resolute, almost of pert appearance, some waiting-maid probably, portrayed in a drawing now in the Windsor Library. Her thin, sharp contours seem to indicate Florentine origin.

Leonardo shows excessive skill in draping his female models and in decking and adorning them. He proves himself in this respect a worthy fellow-disciple of Perugino, who, we are told, was so devotedly attached to his young wife, Clara Fancelli, that he delighted in arranging her dress with his own hands.

The Drapery of the Virgin's Thigh,
c.1515-1517.
Charcoal and black chalk and
white highlights, 16.4 x 14.5 cm.
Royal Library, Windsor Castle.

Drapery Study for the Virgin,
c. 1508-1510.
Black and red chalks, pen and
ink and white highlights,
16.4 x 14.5 cm.
Royal Library, Windsor Castle.

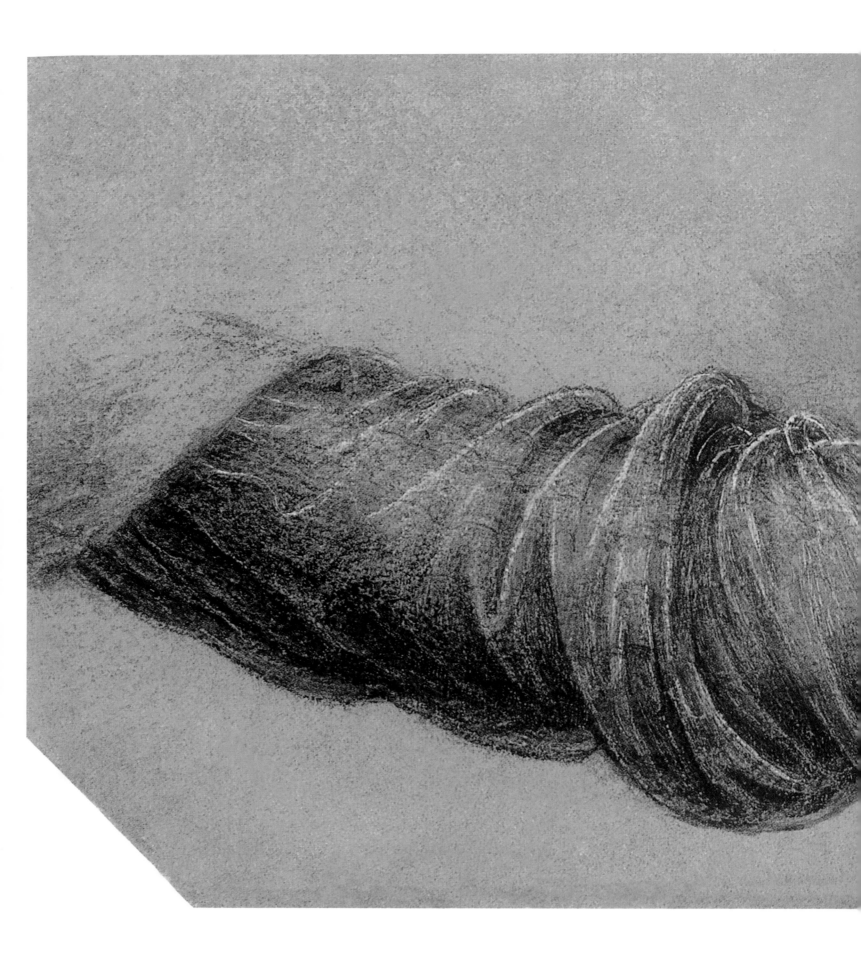

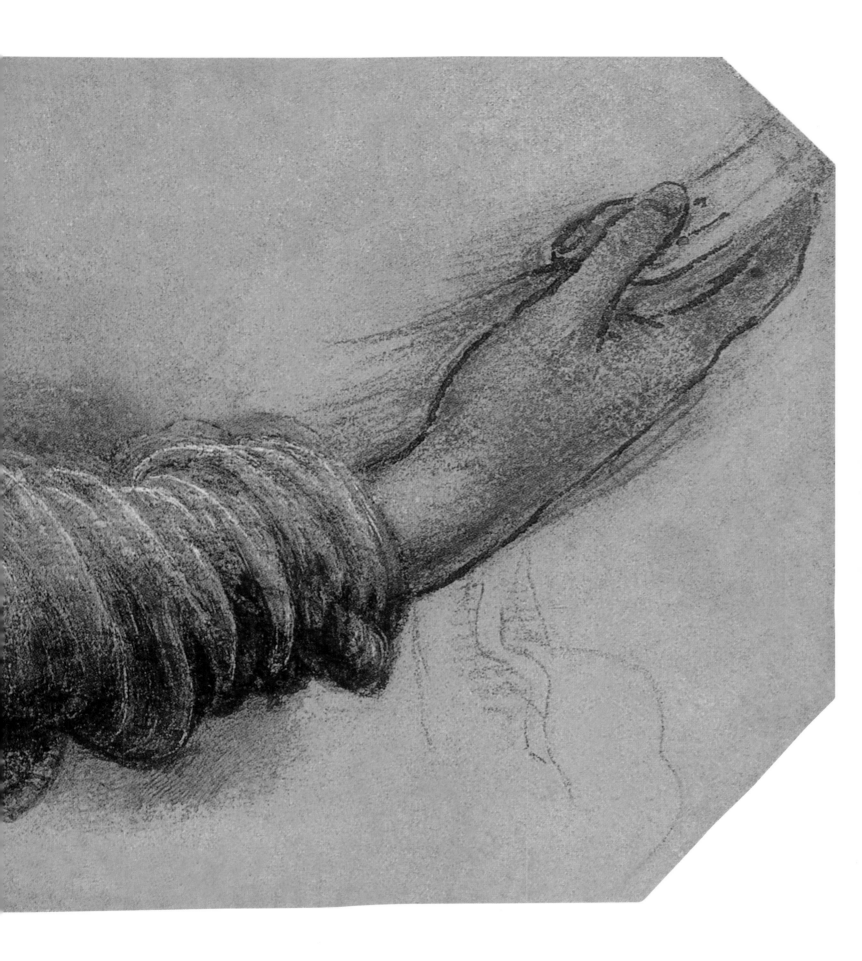

Study for the Head of Leda, 1505.
Pen and wash on black chalk,
17.7 x 14.7 cm.
Royal Library, Windsor Castle.

In the Queen of England's collection at Windsor Castle, Leonardo's studies of the winding and twisting of water as it escapes from a reservoir and those for the plaits of his *Leda*, have been placed in close juxtaposition and not without good reason. The idea of connecting the refinements of fashion with the caprices of nature was one well suited to his sublime fancy.

Later in his life, the artist gradually evolved a kind of ideal costume closely resembling the beautiful simplicity of classic models. In his *Trattato della Pittura*, when treating draperies, he reminds us that a nymph or an angel should be represented in light garments that either swell in the wind or cling close to the body under its action. Then he reveals his inner most thoughts and advises the artist to avoid, as far as possible, any reproduction of the fashions of his own times. *"Fuggire il più che si può gli abiti della sua età."*

The *Saint Anne* in the Louvre (the composition of which was determined in 1501, though not completed until long afterwards) gave the painter an opportunity to show the world his ideal conception of female beauty. At first, as Anatole Gruyer has pointed out in his delightful *Voyage autour du Salon Carré du Louvre*, Leonardo, ignoring the inevitable difference in age between mother and daughter, has shown them both young with the same youth and fair with the same beauty. "Both," adds Gruyer, "are enchantresses with that gift of Italian beauty that is exuberant yet always majestic. They seem compact of light and shadow. The tide of life runs full in their veins, without any taint of vulgar clay and enigmatic, mysterious figures, instinct with a strange depth of sensibility which, while rousing our admiration, fills our souls with an agitation almost paralyzing." A detail of costume must be noted here. The sleeves of the *Saint Anne* are pleated in the same fashion as those of *Mona Lisa:* the two pictures are of the same date, or very near it.

The glorification of saints and martyrs appears to have had but little charm for Leonardo. The Sibyls would have attracted him far more. I cannot but think that he desired to portray one of these mighty and mysterious prophetesses in the tremendous silver-point drawing on green paper preserved in the Louvre Museum: a woman, full face, with great rolling eyes and lips parted as if some prophecy were just about to break from them. Energy and inspiration are pictured here, with indescribable power.

A less startling, but an extraordinarily charming figure is that of a young woman standing in floating draperies, pointing with her left hand at some invisible object. Is this Dante's Beatrice, as has been recently affirmed? The hypothesis is not an unlikely one.

Standing before one of the master's very latest works, that mysterious figure in the Louvre which seems to emerge out of the darkness, bending a face all bathed in light, upon us mortals and raising an arm of matchless modelling towards heaven, a tormenting doubt enters our minds. Is the *St John the Baptist* – such is the title bestowed upon the picture – really man or woman? The voluptuous eyes, the straight delicate nose, the mouth with its bewitching smile, seem to hold a place midway between the half-length cartoon of a nude woman at Chantilly and the *Mona Lisa*. They form a combination of "Apollino", Bacchus and Hermaphroditus.

The years 1504-1505, when Leonardo finished the *Mona Lisa*, mark the apogee of his artistic talent. It was then he revealed his absolute mastery over the resources of his art and notably his possession, to quote the felicitous expression of Charles Blanc, of the secret of modulations in the minor key. Never, before this period or after it, did he carry his feeling for relief further and his triumph is even more brilliant because he obtained his effects by the legitimate resources of painting, without recourse to any of the methods of the sculptor.

It was, in all probability, during his residence in Florence that Leonardo drew the *Triumph of Neptune* on a sheet of paper for his compatriot and intimate friend, Antonio Segni. Vasari praises the extreme finish of this drawing. It showed, he tells us, the stormy sea, the chariot drawn by seahorses, with monsters (*"fantasime"*) grampuses, winds (*"noti"*) and some very fine heads of sea-gods. Fabio, son of Antonio Segni, gave this drawing to Giovanni Gaddi.

The central part of this composition is probably shown in the magnificent drawing from the Windsor Library. No words can describe the life and movement, the intensity, the fancy, overflowing yet restrained expression of this fragment. Every line is melodious, eloquent and triumphant.

We have every reason to suppose that Leonardo was also working at this period on his picture of *Leda*.

Leda

In a recent article in the *Jahrbuch,* Müller-Walde pointed out, on a sheet of the *Codex Atlanticus,* which every student of Leonardo had handled and fingered without discovering anything at all, the painter's original sketch for the lost masterpiece. There can be no doubt about the matter. The sketch, though microscopic in dimensions, contains the germ of the whole idea of the *Leda.* She stands erect, holding in her left arm (the side of the heart) a confused mass that is easily recognizable as Jupiter under the form of a bird.

This drawing, let me remark, proves that the cartoon of the *Leda* was at Florence, where Raphael must have copied it and that it must have been there in 1505 or 1506, for this is the latest date which can be assigned to Raphael's copy.

What has become of the masterpiece? Here, I confess, I see no light. Can Leonardo's creation, in spite of its modesty of treatment, have been cut up, like Correggio's *Leda,* by some devout bigot? Was it lost in some fire? Was it given by Louis XVI to some foreign Sovereign, like the *St John* bestowed by the French monarch on Charles I of England? I refrain, in my complete ignorance, from putting forward any hypothesis whatsoever. I am content to demonstrate, by means of these ancient copies, the comparative accuracy of which I have just proven, with what modest grace, restraint and dignity the master treated a most dubious subject.

Though, during his various residences at Florence between 1500 and 1513, Leonardo does not appear to have used the chisel for any personal creation of his own, he certainly gave his young friend and host, the sculptor Giovanni Francesco Rustici (born 1474, died 1554) the benefit of his advice.

He shared more or less directly in the execution of the group of three bronze statues with which Rustici adorned the Baptistry and which were placed in position in 1511 – *St John the Baptist Preaching Between the Levite and the Pharisee.* According to Vasari, Leonardo's attention was especially given to the preparation of the moulds and to the iron framework intended for the protection of the bronzes and he even worked with his own hands on the models. There can be no doubt about his influence on the work; it is evident in more than one detail. It struggles with that of Donatello and Michelangelo in these three most expressive figures.

From every point of view, Leonardo's residence in Florence was full of trials. He found himself involved in painfully sordid discussions, both as an artist and as a man. When his father died (9 July 1504), his brothers, on the score of his illegitimacy, refused him his share of the inheritance, a portion that, on account of the number of participants, could not have been a large one. The business dragged on and the final division of the property did not take place until 15 April 1506. A matter that must have tried Leonardo even more severely was the attempt made by his brothers, after the death of his uncle Francesco, in 1507, to dispute his possession of the few roods of ground that the latter had expressly bequeathed to him by his will, dated 12 August 1504. This time, in spite of his dislike of business and more especially of lawsuits, he appealed to the Florentine Courts. The suit was still undecided in 1511 and he was forced to seek the aid of the Maréchal de Chaumont, of Louis XII and of the Cardinal d'Este.

Here is Leonardo reduced to the role of petitioner, Leonardo condemned to wait on procurators and judges in order to fight his own brothers, what humiliation for such a proud temperament! Also, more than anything else, the failure to fix the *Battle of Anghiari* upon the wall of the Council Hall filled the artist with disgust for a work that might have kept him in his own city. That is not to say, however, that he abandoned his work spontaneously; the truth is that once he had entered into contact with the Maréchal de Chaumont and Louis XII and been drawn into this new system, he subsequently found it impossible to regain his freedom, and such a temperament as his meant that a work interrupted was a work sacrificed.

So once again, Leonardo turned his face to a foreign country.

After Leonardo da Vinci, *Leda and the Swan,* c. 1515-1520. Tempera on wood panel, 112 x 86 cm. Galleria Borghese, Rome.

V. HIS RETURN TO MILAN AND HIS EXILE IN FRANCE IN THE SERVICE OF FRANCIS I

His Return to Milan

Leonardo's eyes were once more turned to Milan, where the French had established a regular government. What changes had taken place since his last visit!

During his first stay in Milan, Louis XII had already seen and admired the *Last Supper* of Santa Maria delle Grazie and the equestrian statue of Lodovico Sforza. His personal acquaintance with the artist seems, however, to have dated only from 1507, the year in which he again passed the Alps to take possession of revolted Genoa. The ground had been well prepared by Charles d'Amboise, whose admiration for Leonardo passed all bounds. The artist had only to reap what this protector had so generously sown for him.

No sooner had the French King withdrawn, however, to his own country than Leonardo set himself anew to cultivate the friendship of the king's representatives, Florimond Robertet and Charles d'Amboise, to say nothing of his ally, Cæsar Borgia.

On 30 May 1506, he obtained permission from the Florentine government to leave, on the condition that he returned at the end of three months and reported himself to the Signory; default to be punished by a fine of 150 gold ducats. He returned, in fact, more than once to his native city during the autumn of 1507 and the spring of 1509, as well as in 1511, 1513 and, finally, in 1514. However, he gave no more thought to his old commissions. For him, as well as for Soderini and the Medici, the *Battle of Anghiari* was dead and buried.

Another letter from the Maréchal arrived 16 December, in which Charles allows his enthusiasm for Leonardo to break through the terms in which he thanks the Signory for their consent to extend the artist's leave: "The excellent works," he writes, "left in Italy and more especially in Milan, by Master Leonardo da Vinci, your fellow-citizen, have led all those who have seen them to have a singular affection for their author, even when they are personally unacquainted with him. For ourselves, we confess that we were among those who loved him even before our eyes had rested upon him. Now, since we have known him and been much in his company and have had personal experience of his various gifts, we truly see that his name, famous in painting, is relatively obscure so far as those other branches of knowledge in which he has reached so great a height are concerned. It pleases us to confess that in the efforts made by him to respond to no matter what calls we make upon his powers – architectural designs and other things relating to our state – he satisfies us in such a way that not only are we contented with him, but have even conceived an admiration for him. Therefore, as it has pleased you to leave him here all these days to do our will, it would seem to us ungrateful not to give our thanks to you on the occasion of his return into his own country. Thus we thank you as warmly as we can and, if it be fitting to give a man of such talent a recommendation to his fellow citizens, we recommend him to you as strongly as we can and assure you that you can never do anything, in the way of augmenting his fortune or comfort, or those honours to which he has a right, without giving, to us as well as to him, the most lively pleasure and putting us under the greatest obligation to your Magnificences."

For the third time the whilom favourite of Lodovico Sforza and of Cæsar Borgia had exercised the arts of a consummate courtier; he had won the favour of the Maréchal de Chaumont, as a preparation for the conquest of the King of France himself.

A sight of the *Last Supper* had been enough to fascinate Louis. This we know from the letter addressed by the Florentine envoy, Pandolfini, to his government on 7 January 1507: "This morning, when I was in the presence of the most Christian King, his Majesty addressed me, saying 'Your Signory must do me a service. Write to them that I wish to employ their painter, Master Leonardo, who is now in Milan and that I want him to make several things for me. Act in such a way that their lordships will order him to enter my service at once and not to leave Milan before my arrival. He is an excellent master and I desire to have several

Bacchus, 1510-1515.
Wood panel transferred on canvas, 177 x 115 cm.
Musée du Louvre, Paris.

things from his hand. So write at once to Florence, sending me the letter (this is the letter; it will reach you by way of Milan).'

Two days afterwards the King himself addressed the following letter to the Signory: "Louis, by the grace of God, King of France, Duke of Milan, Lord of Genoa, etc. Very dear and close friends: As we have need of Master Leonardo da Vinci, painter to your city of Florence and intend to make him do something for us with his own hand and as we shall soon, God willing, be in Milan, we beg you, as affectionately as we can, to be good enough to allow the said Leonardo to work for us such a time as may enable him to carry out the work we intend him to do. As soon as you receive these letters (we beg you to) write to him and direct that he shall not leave Milan until we arrive there. While he is awaiting us we shall let him know what it is that we desire him to do, but meanwhile write to him in such fashion that he shall by no means leave the city before our arrival; I have already urged your ambassador to write to you in the same sense. You will do us a great pleasure in acting as we desire. Dear and close friends, may our Lord have you in his keeping. Written from Blois, 14 January, 1507. (Signed) Louis. ROBERTET." Addressed: "To our very dear and close friends, allies and confederates, the Priors and perpetual Gonfaloniere of the Signory of Florence."

The year 1507 was distinguished by the French King's triumphal entry into Milan (24 May). Leonardo certainly had a share in the great preparations made to do honour to the occasion.

We see from the correspondence given above that, as early as 1506, Leonardo had sent a small picture to Louis XII – probably a Madonna – and that in 1507 he was at work on another picture for his royal patron. On 20 April of this latter year the Maréchal de Chaumont restored to him, by way of recompense, the vineyard he had received from Lodovico shortly before the fall of that prince.

Unhappily, the pictures painted in 1506 and 1507 have disappeared and we cannot even be sure that any hint of what they were has survived in the master's drawings, or in the more or less faithful, more or less imperfect copies, which have come down to us.

Among those pictures which, without being by the master's own hand, may yet have something to do with the Madonnas painted at about this time, the *Virgin of the Scales* in the Louvre and the *Holy Family* of the Hermitage, may specially be noticed.

The St Petersburg *Holy Family* represents the Virgin seated, holding on her knees the Holy Child, who, with a smile, seeks the maternal breast. The young mother's costume consists of a red robe, lined with light blue and a blue mantle lined with green. To the right stands St Joseph, leaning on a staff and smiling tenderly upon the sacred couple. He wears a white tunic and a brown cloak. To the left, St Catherine reads a book; she wears a grey robe bordered with gold and a red mantle and holds a palm branch in her left hand. Near her we see the wheel, the instrument of her martyrdom. The figures are all half-length, except that of the Child Christ.

This *Holy Family* comes from the Mantua Gallery, which was dispersed after the sack of that city in 1630. It was added to the Russian Imperial collections by Catherine II. Clément de Ris and Woermann are inclined to ascribe it to Cesare da Sesto.

This Hermitage *Holy Family* should be studied in connection with the *Virgin of the Bas-relief*, well known through Forster's engraving. The latter work passed from Woodburn, the dealer, into the collection of Lord Monson, at Gatton Park. It represents the Virgin, the Infant Jesus, little St John, St Joseph and St Zacharias.

In the *Virgin with the Scales*, Mary holds little naked Jesus on her lap. The Archangel Michael, kneeling on one knee, offers him a pair of scales, on which Jesus lays his hands. To the left St Elizabeth caresses little St John, who in turn plays with a lamb. The scene is a grotto, with cleft rocks not unlike those of the *Virgin of the Rocks*. The expressions are uniformly smiling and the scale of tones lacks force and depth. To me it appears doubtful whether even the composition was derived from Leonardo; the picture has been attributed both to Salai and to the mediocre d'Oggiono.

Leonardo was fond of fantastic subjects and was even prone, on occasion, to a treatment that seems to us to border on irreverence. He proposed to paint the Madonna and the Child Jesus playing with a cat. Drawings in which this idea is treated in various ways are numerous.

A theme like this might have led to much in the hands of a virtuoso like Leonardo, but we have no proof that he ever attacked it with the brush.

Profile of Salaï, c. 1510.
Red chalk, 21.7 x 15.3 cm.
Royal Library, Windsor Castle.

The history of the *Bacchus* cannot be traced beyond the seventeenth century. According to Cassiano del Pozzo it was in the Palace at Fontainebleau in 1625.

It does not require much insight to understand that from the time of Leonardo's second stay in Milan the French Court exerted all sorts of pressure to induce him to take up his residence in France. The master refused, however; and the Cardinal d'Amboise, who was then working at the Château de Gaillon, was obliged to make do with one of his disciples Andrea Solario.

We hear, indeed, of a letter addressed to Leonardo in 1509 with this superscription, *"Monsieur Lyonnard, peintre du Roy pour Amboyse."* My learned colleague and friend, Charles Ravaisson-Mollien, is also inclined to believe that the artist sojourned in France between the spring of 1507 and the autumn of 1510. However, Uzielli has successfully refuted this hypothesis.

His lawsuit with his family obliged Leonardo to return to Florence in 1507.

In less than three weeks the King's letter was received, on 15 August 1507; Charles d'Amboise addressed another to the seigniory, urging them to hasten the artist's return:

Most exalted Lords: Master Leonardo da Vinci, painter to his Most Christian Majesty, is on his way to you. As he is engaged on a picture for his Majesty, we have, much against our wills, given him the leave he demanded, in order that he might put an end to certain difficulties which have arisen between himself and his brothers in the matter of a heritage left to him by an uncle. In order that he may return promptly to finish the work he has begun, we beg your Excellencies to lend him all the help and protection that may be just, so that his case and his general affairs may be settled with all possible expedition. In doing this your Excellencies will give pleasure to his Most Christian Majesty and also to ourselves. Given at Milan. In everything yours, D'AMBOISE.

It was at this point that Leonardo began his work on the Lombard canal. In order to open navigation all the way from Milan to Como, it was necessary to prolong the Martesana canal from Tresso to Brivio and to construct two sets of locks of the length of about six and a half miles. Leonardo thought out the scheme (*Cod. Atlan.* fols. 137, 139, 233, 328), which was taken up again in 1519 with variations. The engineer Meda finally put it into execution at the end of the sixteenth century. Mazzenta tells us that in his time the canal was called "the Machine of the French", however, Meda failed to understand the economy of Leonardo's scheme. Venturi tells us that, in his time, many improvements had been added to the original work.

Louis XII rewarded his artist-engineer with a permit to take twelve "ounces" of water from the main canal at San Cristoforo, a measure that, according to Venturi, corresponds to a waterway of some importance.

Unfortunately, he had long to wait before he obtained any benefit from this privilege. Around 1511, he found himself obliged to address a very pressing letter to the Maréchal de Chaumont, in which, among other things, he says:

I suspect that my feeble recognition of the great benefits I have received from your Excellency has indisposed you towards me and that is why so many letters addressed by me to your lordship have never had an answer. Today I am sending Salai to inform your lordship that my litigation with my brothers is nearing its end and that I hope to be in Milan by Easter. I shall bring with me two pictures of the Madonna, different in size, intended for the Most Christian King: or for anyone else that your lordship may choose. I shall be glad to know where I am to fix my habitation when I return, as I wish no longer to incommode your Excellency. I should also like to know besides, having worked for the Most Christian King, whether my pension is to continue or not. I am writing to the President about the right of water the King gave me. I have never yet been put in enjoyment of the privilege, because at the time there was not much water in the canal in consequence of the great drought and because the openings had not been regulated. But he promised that I should be put in possession as soon as the regularization had been made. I pray your lordship, then, to be good enough to take the trouble, now that the openings are regulated, to remind the President of my rights, so that I may get the said water; for I hope, when I come, to make machines and other things that will give great pleasure to our Most Christian King. I have nothing more to tell you. I am always at your orders.

Nude Study, 1508-1511.
Royal Library, Windsor Castle.

The Bust of a Man, Full Face, and the Head of a Lion,
c. 1505-1510.
Red chalk and white highlights on paper, 18.3 x 13.6 cm.
Royal Library, Windsor Castle.

Study of an Old Man, c. 1505.
Red chalk, 9.4 x 6 cm.
Musée du Louvre, Paris.

Aurelio Luini attributed,
Profile of an Old Man,
16ᵗʰ century.
Metalpoint, pen and ink,
13 x 10.2 cm.
Biblioteca Reale, Turin.

Master of the Pala Sforzesca,
Profile of an Old Man, c. 1495.
Silverpoint on paper,
15 x 11.5 cm.
Galleria degli Uffizi, Florence.

In another letter, addressed to Francesco Melzi, Leonardo returns to these same claims, which were in the end satisfied.

Once more, in 1509, Louis XII wrote his name large on the Fasti of Milan, which, at that time, contained many brilliant pages. Once more, on 1 May, he made a "*Joyeuse Entrée*" into the ancient capital of the Visconti and the Sforzi. It is said that the master of the ceremonies was no other than Leonardo and that the preparations took no less than forty-six days. The king then passed eight days in Milan. He returned there on 1 July, when, as the conqueror of Agnadel, he was received with still greater magnificence.

The artistic and scientific labours of Da Vinci were interrupted now and then by excursions into the country around Milan, especially to Vaprio, situated at some distance from the capital, between Gorgonzola and Bergamo, on the Adda, where Melzi had a property. We know that he was there on the 5 July 1507, for on that day he thence addressed a long letter to his stepmother, his sister and stepsister. The letter is addressed from "the Canonry of Vaprio."

Maximilian, moreover, did not long enjoy this return of fortune. In 1513, his subjects revolted on the approach of the French. Nonetheless, his power seemed to be restored in 1513 after the rout of Louis XII at Novara, the defeat of Marignano put an end to his domination two years later. He was obliged to renounce his rights over Milan and, like so many of Leonardo's friends and protectors, like Lodovico Sforza, Trivulzio, the sculptor Rustici, he ended his days in France. He died in Paris in 1530.

Once again, Leonardo had to seek a new protector and a fresh asylum, which he found in Rome, in the service of Pope Leo X.

A political revolution drove Leonardo from Milan. Another, more pacific in character, sent him to seek his fortune in Rome. Julius II, the soldier Pope, who was accustomed to entering

towns through the holes he had battered in their walls, was succeeded on 11 March, 1513, by Giovanni de' Medici, son of the great Lorenzo and inheritor of long-established traditions of luxury and taste, who took the name Leo X. No sooner had the choice of the Conclave become known than, from near and far, all who prided themselves on their artistic ability – architects, sculptors, painters: Fra Bartolommeo, Sodoma, Signorelli, and Timoteo Viti – hastened to the precincts of the Vatican.

Leonardo assumed that a Sovereign Pontiff with a passionate love of the arts would give a cordial welcome to a compatriot and former protégé of his father, Lorenzo; and he at once set out for Rome. He may have made the acquaintance of the Cardinal de' Medici, the future Leo X, during his captivity in Milan after the battle of Ravenna.

In one of his notes, the master lets us know that he left Milan for Rome on 24 September 1513, accompanied by Giovanni, Francesco Melzi, Salai, Lorenzo and Fanfoja. The presence of Michelangelo, Leonardo's ancient enemy, may have struck a bad note in the general harmony, but he could not hurt da Vinci's interests, for his own star was, for the moment, in eclipse.

The Ambrosiana at Milan, so rich in false Leonardo drawings, possesses an old man's portrait in red chalk, with energetic features and an expression at once sarcastic and morose. This drawing I ascribe with some confidence to Leonardo, in spite of an air with which the critic might reasonably find fault. The thing I wish to point out about it is not so much the subtle vigour of the execution, as a certain family likeness, as it were, to a figure in one of the frescos in the Hall of Constantine, in the Vatican. Long ago, when studying the fresco that represents Leo X approving the plans of the new St Peter's, I was struck with the presence of a bald and bearded individual in the middle of the composition, standing with an air of remarkable assurance, unrolling Bramante's plans for the great undertaking. The fresco, no doubt, has been

Profile of an Old Man (Gian Giacomo Trivulzio?), c. 1510.
Black and red chalk,
22.2 x 16 cm.
Royal Library, Windsor Castle.

Profile of an Old Man Crowned with Bay Leaves, c. 1506-1508.
Pen and ink, red chalk on paper,
16.8 x 12.5 cm.
Biblioteca Reale, Turin.

more than half repainted, but an old engraving by Pietro Santi Bartoli is sufficient evidence that the heads have not been altered in their essential features.

Leo X welcomed Leonardo with great cordiality and gave him lodging in the Belvedere itself. There we find him installed in December 1513.

The story goes that when the Pope had given him a commission for a picture, Leonardo began at once to distil herbs and oils in order to make the varnish, whereupon Leo exclaimed, "Alas! This man will do nothing, for he begins to think about the finishing of his picture before he gives a thought to the commencement!" (Vasari)

In Rome, the chemist and physicist completely eclipsed the painter. At one time we find Leonardo writing a paper on the striking of coins for the Pope's mint, at another he is trying experiments in what may be called the comic side of physics. He gave himself up, says Vasari, to innumerable follies of the latter kind, trifling with mirrors and making all sorts of strange experiments, in the desire to find oils for painting and varnishes with which to preserve pictures.

Leonardo's stay in Rome seems to have been interrupted by several excursions. On 25 September, 1514, we find him at Parma; but he was soon back on the Tiber, as we gather from a letter addressed to his brother Giuliano by his sister-in-law Lesandra (Alessandra) on 14 December. Writing from Florence to Rome, Lesandra charges her husband to recall her to Leonardo, a unique and excellent man: *"Mi rachomandiate a votro fratello Leonardo, uomo excellentissimo e singhularissimo."*

Leonardo did not wait for the departure of his patron Giuliano before quitting the Eternal City. Giuliano, as we know from Leonardo himself, left Rome on 9 January 1515; on the same day – the painter adds – the King of France died.

On 9 December 1515 at the latest, Leonardo again found himself in Milan, for on that day he wrote to his steward ("*castaldo*") Zanobi Boni, to point out, for the benefit of the Fiesolan vineyards, certain improvements in the making of wine.

Did Leonardo take part in the competition set afoot by Leo X for the façade of San Lorenzo, at Florence? Nothing is more unlikely. Not only did he never do anything to recommend himself as an architect to the Pope, but he had quit Rome and Florence for the north before 1516, when the competition began.

This was the last time he ever set foot in his native city.

Leonardo's Final Days working under Francis I and his Great Influence

On 13-14 September 1515, Francis I won the victory of Marignano and on 16 October he made his triumphal entry into Milan. This time Leonardo again stood in the forefront of those who had assembled to greet the rising sun.

From Milan, Francis I proceeded to Bologna where Pope Leo X awaited him. Leonardo probably followed close on the King's heels. (He can hardly have been at Bologna on 11 or 12 December, the date of the French king's arrival in the city, for we know him to have been in Milan on the ninth.)

One thing is certain, that at some moment the maestro painted the portrait of "Messire Artus, master of the king's chamber" – a bald and beardless old man, with a hooked nose and projecting chin.

To the same period, if I am not mistaken, belong those heads of strange-looking old men, of which Leonardo has left us such a large variety. Their resemblance to the portrait of *Messire Artus* warrants this assertion. On 22 December, Leo X was back in Florence and Francis I was journeying to his own dominions. From that time onward Leonardo did not leave the victor of Marignano. Giuliano de' Medici was still alive (he died in Florence on 17 March 1516), but the artist had quit his service some considerable time before.

The idea of youth is so closely connected with the radiant genius of Leonardo that it seems to affect every part of his long career. While no master ever suffered less from the uncertainties and disappointments of his earlier days, none assuredly ever knew less of the weakness and failure of old age. The freshness of his impressions, the vivacity of his style, the

Self Portrait, c. 1512.
Red chalk on paper,
33.3 x 21.3 cm.
Biblioteca Reale, Turin.

eternal smile which he wore until the very last, would make us fancy he was never more than twenty, just as his rival, Michelangelo, seems always to have been sixty. It is as hard to imagine Leonardo aged, gloomy and infirm, as it is to conceive Michelangelo young and gay. When more than sixty years have passed over his head, he resolved, with a cheerful heart, to cross the Alps, convinced he would be able to satisfy all the fancies of the young and eager king. A few days before his death he was still taking intricate notes with all the eagerness of youth. What for, ye gods, unless it was to act upon them in the next world?

With all its generous aspirations, the personification of that springtide of human intelligence, crushed in the blossom by religious struggles (even as Michelangelo personifies the spirit of revolt, the melancholy and the pain of belief, threatened by science and of morality, sacrificed by artists and scholars) may we not take Leonardo as the incarnation of the Renaissance?

Francis I showed his desire to honour the greatness of the master by bestowing a princely revenue upon him – 700 crowns. Benvenuto Cellini, who boasted, at a later date, that he had been granted a like sum, attests this fact.

As that great man's genius was as vast as it was varied and as he had a certain acquaintance with Greek and Latin literature, King Francis, who was violently enamoured of his great talents, took so great a delight in hearing him argue, that he only parted from him for a few days in the year, thus preventing him from putting the splendid studies, which he had carried on with so much discipline, to actual use. I must not fail to repeat the words concerning him

St John the Baptist, 1513-1515.
Oil on canvas, 69 x 57 cm.
Musée du Louvre, Paris.

The Incarnate Angel,
c. 1513-1514.
Private collection, Germany.

that I heard from the king's own lips, when he spoke to me, in the presence of the Cardinal of Ferrara, the Cardinal of Lorraine and the King of Navarre. He affirmed that never any man had come into the world who knew so much as Leonardo; and that not only in matters of sculpture, painting and architecture, for in addition, he was a great philosopher.

The residence assigned to Leonardo was in the good town of Amboise, the cradle of the first colony of artists summoned to France by Charles VIII and the favourite dwelling-place of the young reigning monarch. There a great part of his youth had been spent; there, in the first year of his reign, he had celebrated the betrothal of Renée de Montpensier with the Duke of Lorraine; there, between 1515 and 1517, three of his own children were born.

Leonardo was assigned the little manor house of Cloux, standing between the castle and the town of Amboise. This residence, built by Etienne le Loup, steward of Louis XI, had been bought in 1490, with all the lands attached to it, by Charles VIII for the sum of 3,500 gold crowns. It had afterwards passed into the hands of the Comte de St Pol; thence into those of the Duc d'Alençon and finally, into the possession of Queen Louise de Savoie, mother of Francis I. The manor house, now known under the name of Clos-Lucé, has been tastefully restored.

"The house, built of brick and white stone, has a sunny aspect and is sheltered on the north by the hill. It consists of two *corps de logis,* forming a square. In the inner angle of this square rises an elegant winding staircase, of octagonal shape. Leonardo," says Anatole de Montaiglon, from whom I borrow this description, "has leant on the window sills of the two storeys, his feet have trodden the staircase, his step has passed through all the eight large rooms of which the dwelling is composed; and in the quiet house, which has not altered, externally at least, since those days, we can imagine we see him yet." We are assured that the room in which he breathed his last is still in existence, with its raftered ceiling, its huge hearth and its general aspect of austerity.

The aged and illustrious painter described his residence as a palace. "24 June, St John's Day," 1518, at Amboise, nel palazzo del Clli. (sic)" is the entry in his own hand in one of his notebooks.

The wonderful little *St John the Baptist* in the Louvre is certainly one of Leonardo's last works. It is a proof that his noble intelligence was constantly rising higher and that the flame burnt brightest just before it was finally quenched.

A vision, a dream, a kind of impalpable image of a head and arm, rising out of a mysterious penumbra – such is this enchanting picture. So delicate and tender are the features that the artist must certainly have taken them from a female model, imitating, in this particular, several of his Florentine predecessors and, notably, Donatello and Agostino di Duccio, the sculptor of the church of St Francis, at Rimini. These two artists seem to have taken delight in modelling androgynous figures. On representations of St John, the patron saint of Florence, the Primitives, from Donatello onwards, lavished every seduction of their art, every skilful caress, as it were, of brush or chisel. For the ascetic type of him who lived on locusts and wild honey, they substituted a beautiful beardless youth, starting out on his desert journey, full of hope and pleasurable expectation. The delicate modelling of the arm and raised hand, in the Louvre picture, defy all description. The expression of the face, with its exquisite smile and airy grace, is ineffable, to say nothing of the miraculous execution of the picture and the knowledge of chiaroscuro, so profound that Rembrandt seems to have borrowed its secrets from Leonardo. Compare the two painters' methods. They are identical – to bring a figure into relief against the penumbra of the background and make it participate in the mysterious illumination. In this particular, the *St John the Baptist* and the *Night Watch* are twin works, in so far as idealism and realism can resemble one another.

Of all the painters who came after Leonardo, Rembrandt is, in fact, the one who approaches nearest to him, both in his indecision as regards literary painting and very plastic formulae and his magic treatment of chiaroscuro.

Some short time after this visit, the masterpiece passed into the collection of King Francis I; Louis XIII presented it to Charles I of England, in exchange for Holbein's *Erasmus and a Holy Family* by Titian. It was bought by Jabach at the sale of Charles I's pictures, for the ridiculously small sum of £140 and was made over to Louis XIV by the famous banker. Since that time it has remained in the national collection of France.

Study of a Torso, c. 1511.
Red chalk, 12 x 14.3 cm.
Royal Library, Windsor Castle.

The aged artist had to face more than one disappointment. The first of these was owing to the unprepared condition of his foreign hosts and neighbours. Why should we hesitate to admit the fact? France was not ripe for the teaching, artistic or scientific, of this pre-eminent representative of the new school of thought and the influence that the gifted leader should have exercised on French art in general and the artists of Touraine in particular, was reduced to little or nothing. The time was past when the valiant chief of the School of Tours, Jean Fouquet, had gone to Italy, to assimilate the conquests of the Renaissance. Flemish influence and a kind of inertia, had laid a paralysing hand on French painters. Leonardo was too worn out to resume, among insufficiently prepared pupils, a work of initiation that in his hands would have been crowned with very different success from that it earned in those of such decadent artists as il Rosso, Primaticcio and Niccolo dell'Abbate. We have no proof, indeed, that the French painters felt themselves at all attracted by a style that was far too transcendent for their commonplace natures.

Not that the master's reputation had failed to reach the banks of the Seine, the Loire and the Rhone.

The very superiority of his genius discouraged his new fellow-citizens and divided them from him. Among the few French artists who were influenced more or less directly by Leonardo, the place of honour must be allotted to the engraver Geoffroy Tory, of Bourges. In his *Champ Fleury* (1529), he speaks of the Italian artist in terms of high praise.

Francis I, as we know by Leonardo's certificate of burial, had engaged his services, not as his painter only, but as his engineer, architect and mechanic.

A Male Anatomical Figure showing the Viscera and Principle Vessels, c. 1490-1493. Pen and ink with wash over black chalk, 28 x 19.8 cm. Royal Library, Windsor Castle.

The Female Sexual Organs, c. 1509. Pen and ink on charcoal and traces of red chalk with bistre wash, 46.7 x 33.2 cm. Royal Library, Windsor Castle.

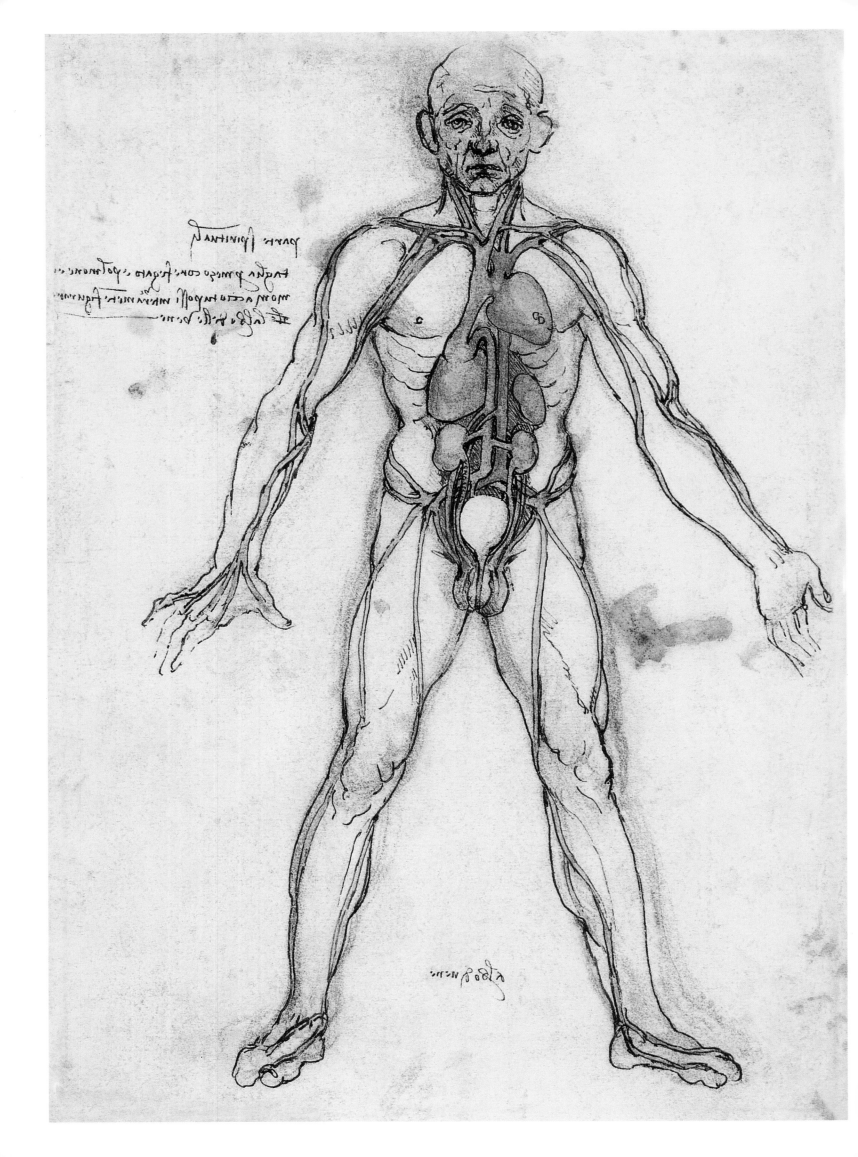

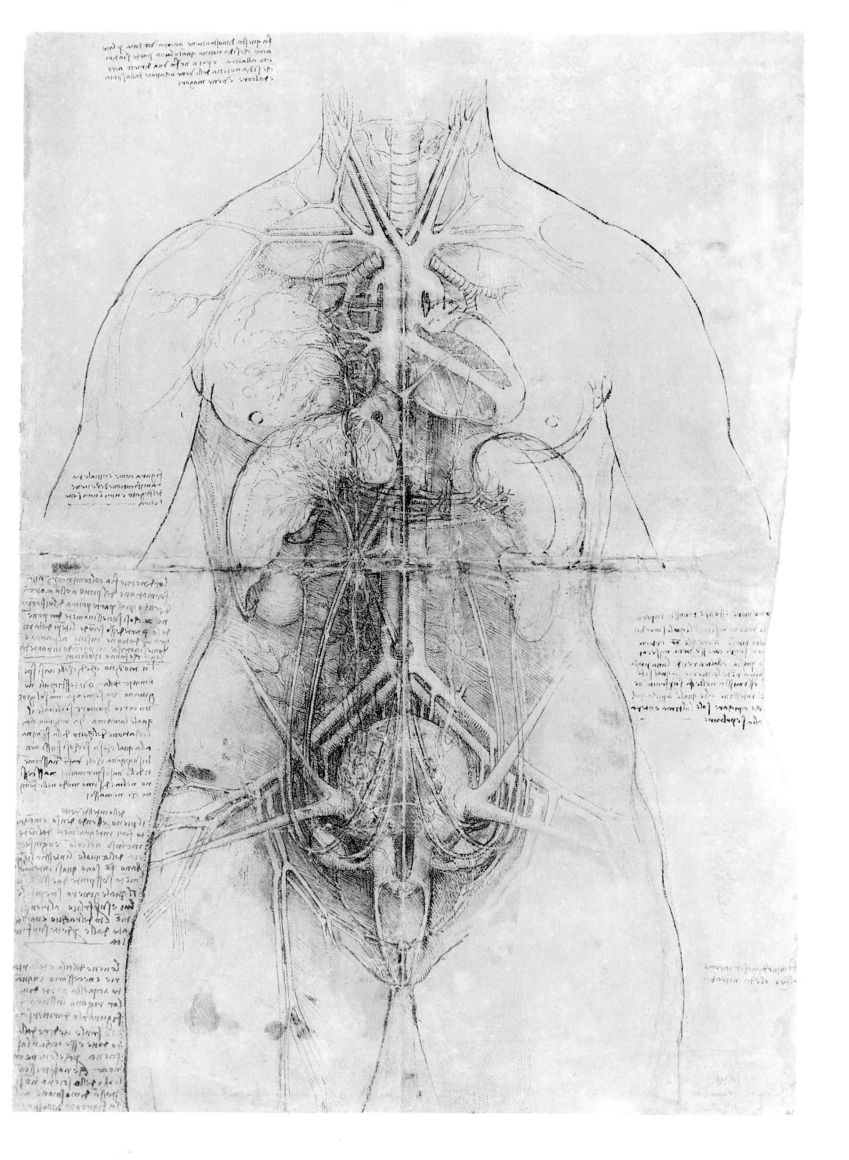

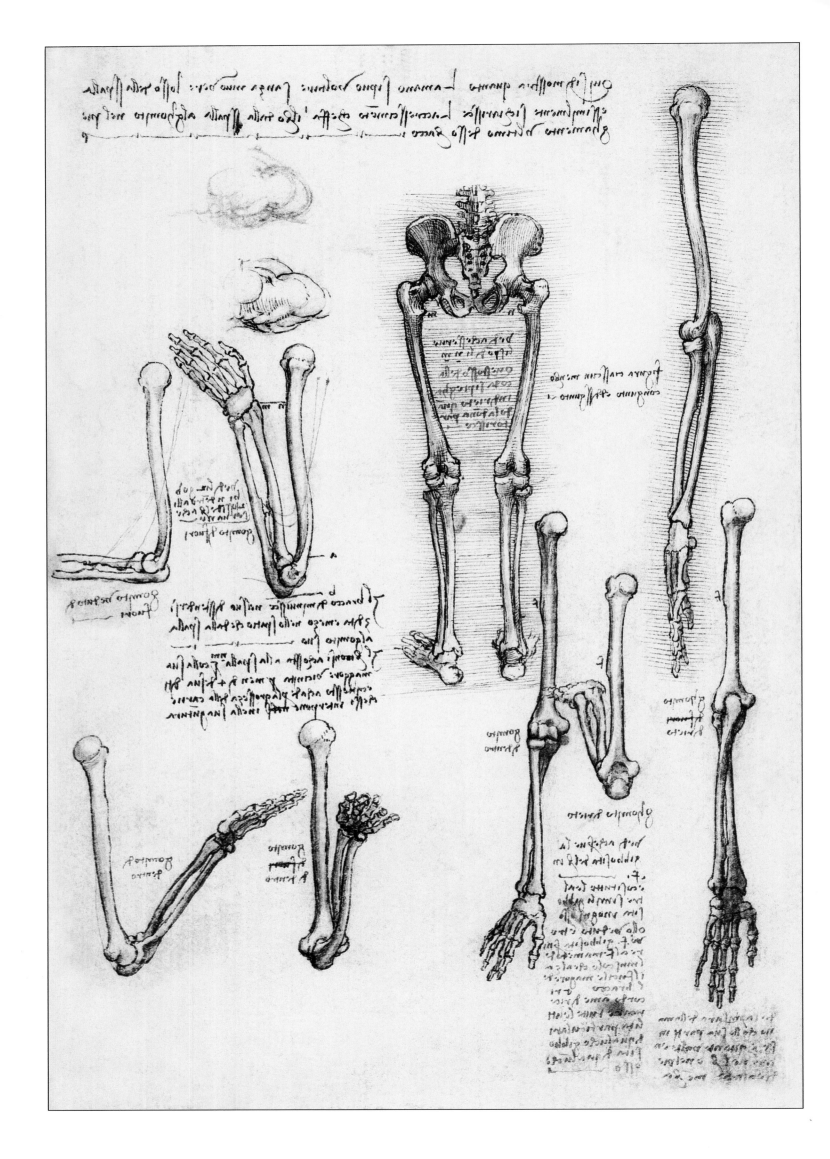

On the occasion of an excursion to Blois, Leonardo was much interested in the canal and irrigation works carried out there, some twenty or twenty-five years previously, by his fellow-countryman Fra Giocondo, the learned Veronese monk.

In connection with this residence in Touraine, we have a sketch that is evidently the plan for a house to be built beside the road leading to Amboise, with a huge hollowed out space near it, surrounded by tiers of seats for spectators.

Leonardo also seems to have collected information as to the conditions of the tide at Bordeaux.

Did women claim any share in the latest thoughts of the aged artist? A passage in his will would almost lead us to think so. Amongst his legatees is a poor woman of the humblest sort, a servant, old and ugly, in all probability. "Item, I leave my servant Mathurine a gown of good black cloth, trimmed with fur, a cloth cloak and two ducats, to be paid her once only and this also to reward the faithful service of the said Mathurine, until this day."

The clause in the will refers, no doubt, to some prosaic housekeeper belonging to the province, whom Leonardo had taken into his service when he settled at Amboise. Thus, to his latest hour, the artist who created so many and such matchless female types – virgins, mothers, matrons, prophetesses and sibyls – seems, by some strange contradiction, to have banished the sex from his own inmost existence and denied it all communion with the sublime secrets of his thoughtful and poetic soul.

This independence of all female affection explains the ease with which the master moved from one home to another, leaving Florence for Milan and Milan for Florence, following the fortunes of Cæsar Borgia, of the Maréchal d'Amboise, of Giuliano de' Medici, of Francis I of France and venturing, at last, when over sixty years of age, to try his fortune beyond the mountains.

Leonardo's health had been declining for some considerable time already. The numbness or paralysis that affected his right hand was but the premonitory symptom of worse troubles. The noble old man thought it well to make his last arrangements. The fine maxim he had himself composed: "As a well-spent day ensures happy slumbers, so does a well-spent life ensure a happy death." A week before his death, he sent for Maître Boreau, an Amboise notary, whose descendants carried on his business until 1885 and dictated his will to him.

The original will is lost; but Scribe, a professor at the college of Romorantin, had the good fortune of finding an old copy of the Italian text, dating from the seventeenth century and bearing every sign of scrupulous exactitude.

This copy enables us, in the first place, to solve a serious chronological problem. The will is dated 23 April 1518 and it was a question whether the year was to be reckoned on the Italian system (in Rome, for instance, it began on 25 December and sometimes on 1 January), or on the French one – that is to say, from Easter. It has been contended that 1518 was the correct date.

However, the learned Turinese professor overlooked the fact that in the will the date was preceded by the words "before Easter". In the notice prefixed by Anatole de Montaiglon to Scribe's publication, this valuable entry is not allowed to escape reference. In 1518, Easter Day fell on 4 April. In 1519, it was on 24 April. The correctness of this latter date is therefore definitely established.

This document shows us that Leonardo's fortune consisted, at the time of his death, of the vineyard at Milan, the 400 florins deposited at Santa Maria Novella, his rights in the Canal of St Christopher at Milan and his yearly pension.

A codicil to the document is supposed to have existed and Melzi's letter does certainly affirm that Leonardo bequeathed his little property at Fiesole to his brothers, a legacy which does not appear in the will itself. Melzi adds that he does not know whether or not there was another will (evidently of previous date).

The last surviving member of the Boreau family assured Arsène Houssaye that the will had been drawn up in French. This assertion is anything but improbable. Leonardo probably dictated it in Italian, for we have no reason to believe he acquired the French language during the few years he spent at Amboise. His two fellow-countrymen, who, with Melzi, were present at the drawing up of the instrument, Brother Francesco of Cortona and Brother Francesco of Milan, doubtless translated his directions, as he gave them.

Anatomical Studies of Pelvis, Coccyx and Lower Limb of a Female and Study of Rotation of Arms, c. 1509-1510.
Pen and brown wash and black chalk, 28.6 x 19.3 cm.
Royal Library, Windsor Castle.

The will confirms Vasari's story in one essential point. "At last," writes the biographer, "Leonardo, growing old, fell sick for many months and seeing death draw near, he desired to be carefully instructed concerning the things of our good and holy Christian and Catholic religion and having made his confession and repented with many tears, he insisted, though he could not stand upright and had to be supported in the arms of his friends and servants, on leaving his bed to receive the most blessed Sacrament."

I may point out, parenthetically, that certain formulae in the will, such as the commendation of the testator's soul to "Monseigneur St Michel," a saint who was far more popular with Frenchmen than Italians, may very well have been the work of the notary rather than of Leonardo himself. Further we may ask whether the arrangements made to ensure as much pomp as possible in the funeral ceremonies may not have been more a last flicker of worldly vanity than a sudden reawakening of religious sentiment.

"The king," Vasari goes on, "who often went to see him in the friendliest fashion, arrived at this moment. Leonardo, out of respect, raised himself up in his bed, explained the nature and changes of his illness to him and told him, further, how much he had offended God and men by not using his talent as he should have done (*"non avendo operato nell' arte come si conveniva."*) Just at this moment he was seized with a spasm, the forerunner of death; the king rose from his seat and took hold of his head to help him and prove his favour to him, so as to comfort him in his suffering; but this divine spirit, recognizing that he could never attain a greater honour, expired in the king's arms, at the age of seventy-five (sixty-seven) years, on 2 May 1519."

Modern critics agree in casting doubt on this anecdote, which sheds more honour on Francis I than on Leonardo and which has been the subject of endless pictures, besides those of Ingres, Jean Gigoux and Robert Fleury.

In the first place, it is objected, Melzi makes no reference to the circumstance in his letter informing Leonardo's brothers of his master's death; in the second, Lomazzo asserts that it was Melzi who announced the death to Francis I, a proof that the monarch was not present; and further, the King was not at Amboise, but at St Germain-en-Laye, as appears from a decree given in that place 1 May 1519. This last fact is the most convincing to me. Aimé Champollion, the Marquis de Laborde and Arsène Houssaye maintain, however, that the decree in question may very well have been sealed by the Chancellor in the King's absence; and the fact of his absence on 3 May, the day after that of Leonardo's death, is apparently established.

Anatole de Montaiglon has brought out the real moral of Vasari's story. The King, he says, was in the habit of visiting Leonardo when he was at Amboise. Why should not this kindness to a sick man, so eminently human in its character, be a fact? It may not have been Vasari who embroidered the story and touched up the dramatic effect. That may have been the work of those through whom it reached him.

Thus, he died the mighty genius, full of years and glory, but far from his own land. He had carried the art of painting to its highest perfection and had penetrated further into the mysteries of Nature than any mortal since the days of Epicurus and Aristotle.

The burial took place at Amboise, in the cloister of the church of the Royal Chapter of St Florentin, as we learn from the following document, discovered by Harduin:

"Fut inhumé dans le cloistre de cette église, Messire Lionard de Vincy, nosble millanais, premier peinctre et ingénieur et architecte du Roy, meschasnischien d'estat, et anchien directeur de peincture du Duc de Millan. Ce fut faict le douc^e jour d'aoust, 1519."

("Was buried in the cloister of this church, Messire Lionard de Vincy, milanese noble, first painter and engineer and architect to the King, state mechanic, and former director of painting to the Duke of Milan. This was done the twelfth day of August, 1519.")

France, which showed the artist so much hospitality during his lifetime – which was the first to bring his *Trattato della Pittura* to the light and which is, to this day, the proud possessor of the most extraordinary and rarest collection of his pictures and his manuscripts – has not shown the respect that was their due to Leonardo's earthly remains.

Organs of Respiration, Swallowing and Speaking, c. 1510. Pen and brown wash on black chalk, 29 x 19.6 cm. Royal Library, Windsor Castle.

The Heart, c. 1512-1513. Pen and ink on blue paper, 41 x 28 cm. Royal Library, Windsor Castle.

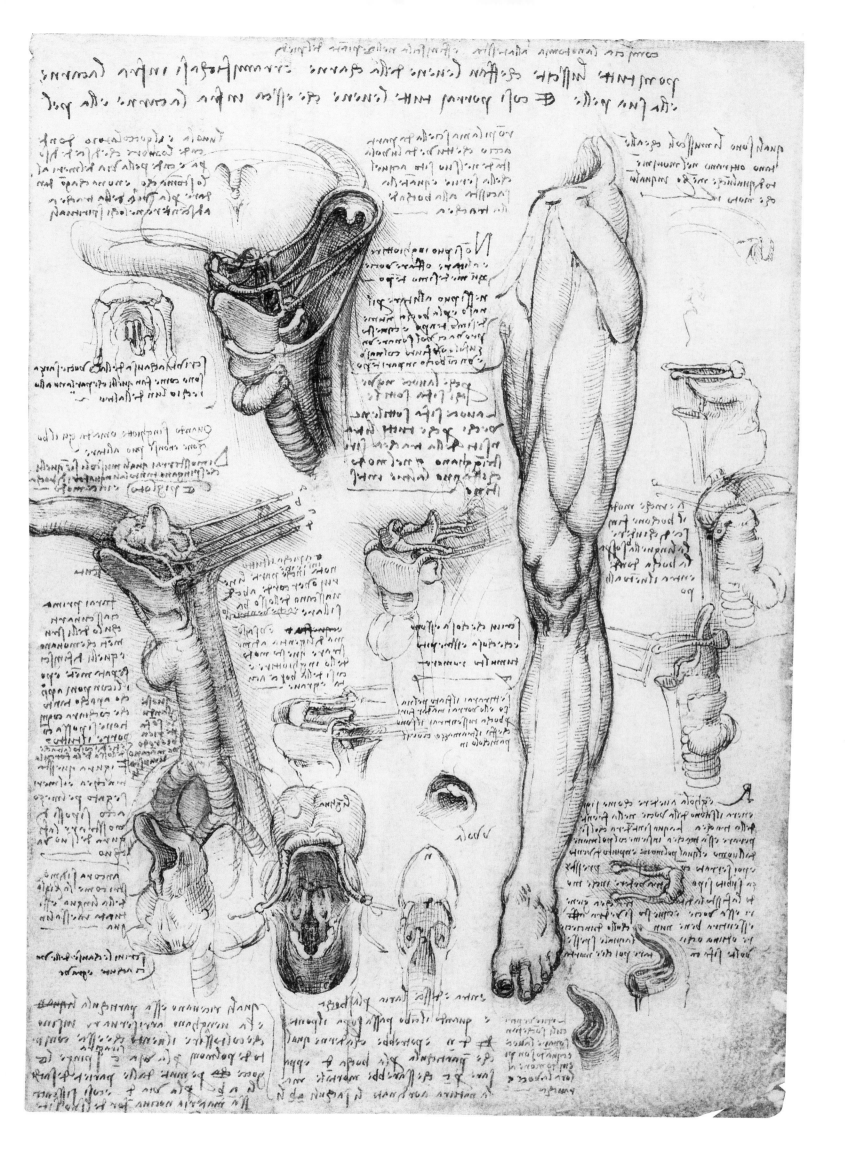

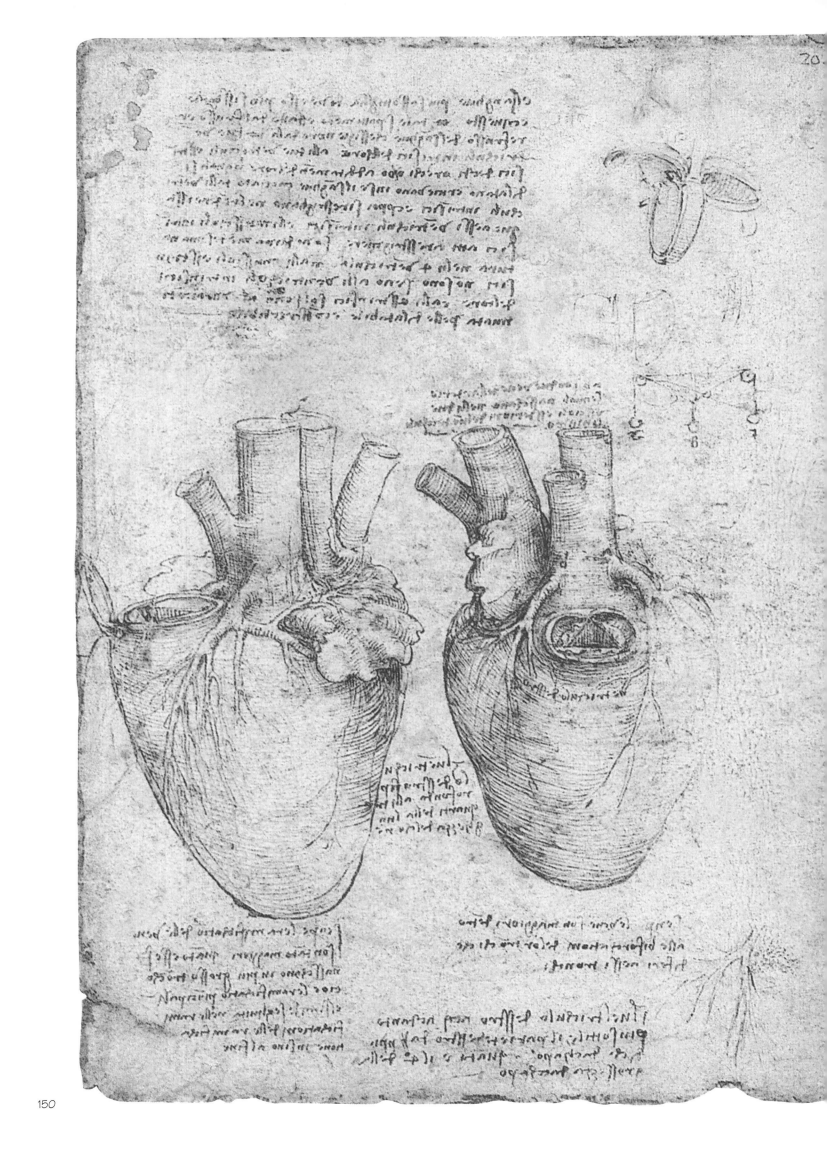

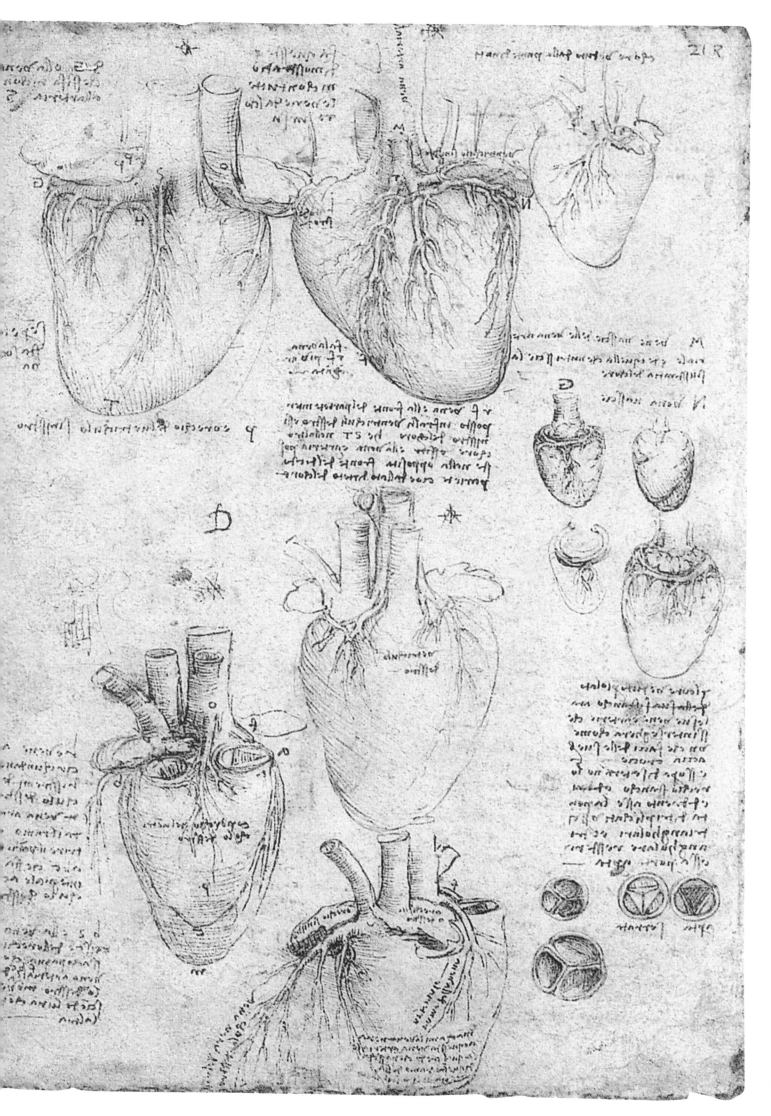

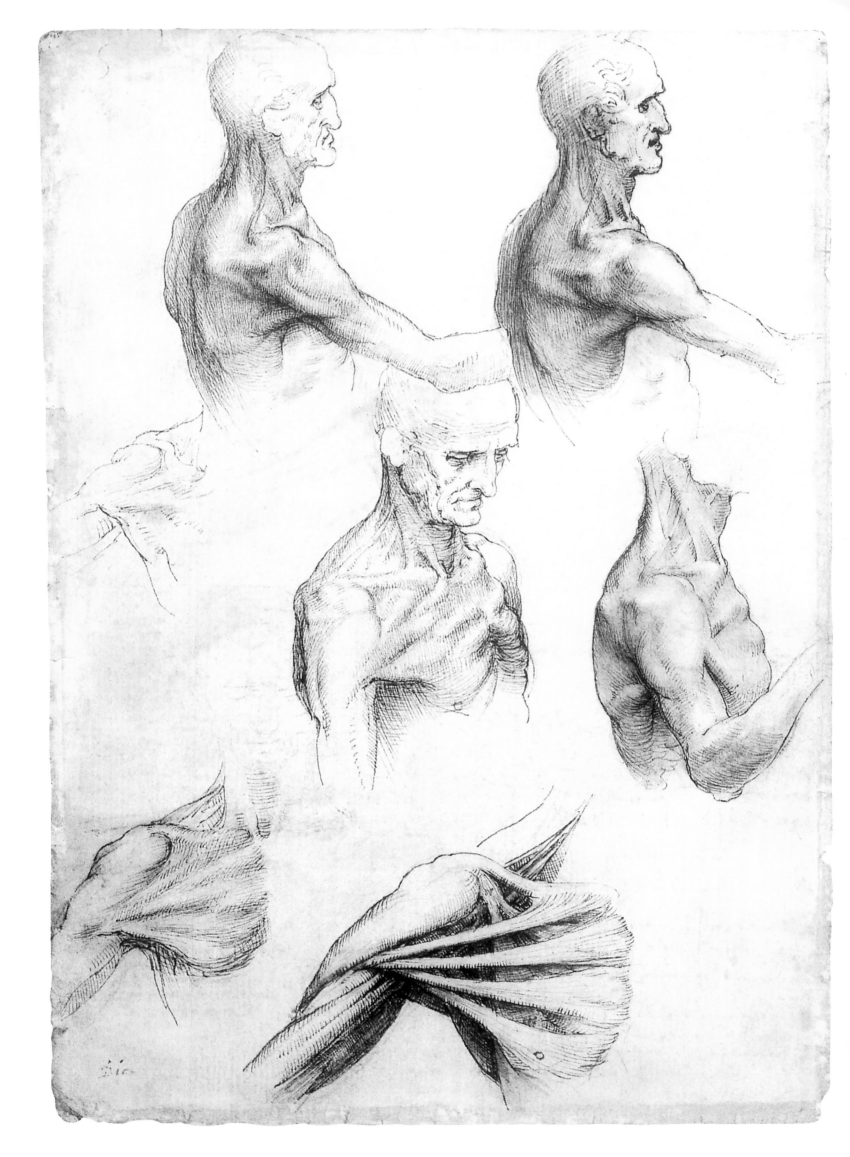

The grave in the church of St Florentin was so soon forsaken and forgotten that we are ignorant of its whereabouts. The century, which gave such gorgeous funerals to Raphael and to Michelangelo, seems to have paid no heed to the passing of their great rival, Leonardo.

The faithful Melzi announced the sad event to Leonardo's family in words of deep feeling. His letter proves him to have possessed a noble heart:

SER JIULIANO AND HIS MOST HONOURABLE BROTHERS,

I think you are apprised of the death of Master Leonardo, your brother and to me even as the best of fathers. I could never express the sorrow it has caused me; and as long as my limbs hang together, I shall suffer from it perpetually and very justly so, because he daily showed me most devoted and warm affection. All men have deplored the loss of such a man as this who is now no longer in life. May the all-powerful God give him eternal peace! He left this present life on 2 May, with all the 'Sacraments of our Holy Mother the Church' and well prepared.

Thanks to the exactness of these notes, we can imagine the appearance of the man who created so many masterpieces. His moral character is equally well known to us.

Let us conjure up the figure of a youth, grave and fascinating at once, a good conversationalist, a celebrated improvisator, a little fond, perhaps, of mystifying his audience, but eager whenever he found himself alone in his inquiries into the most complex intellectual questions. Modesty was not exactly his strong point. The programme he laid before Lodovico il Moro proves that clearly. An extreme gentleness, an exquisite kindliness, fortunately tempered his legitimate confidence in his own powers. His patience with his pupils, one of whom was an ill-conditioned fellow who caused him endless trouble, was almost angelic. He showed tenderness even to unreasoning creatures and would buy caged birds for the sake of the pleasure of setting them free.

Is there any picture of Leonardo as a young man? I would fain believe it. Yet I have sought in vain for any that might seem likely to be his portrait. Let us, while hoping some other inquirer may be more fortunate, content ourselves with the studies by the master's own hand, which represent him in his riper manhood and old age.

Francesco Melzi has already been introduced to my readers. No less dear to him was Salai. "At Milan Leonardo da Vinci took as his pupil one Salai, a Milanese remarkable for his beauty and grace, with beautiful curling and wavy hair, which Leonardo greatly loved and taught him many things pertaining to his art. Several works ascribed in Milan to Salai were touched up by Leonardo." This, if I am not mistaken, is all we know of the life history of the young Salai, or Salaino.

Andrea Salai (the diminutive of Salaino) first makes his appearance in 1495. He fulfilled the duties of "garzone" (almost those of a servant) about Leonardo's person. (The intimacy existing in those days between master and man imparted a dignity, which has now well nigh disappeared, to all domestic service.) His master's extreme indulgence permitted him to gratify a tolerably extravagant taste.

In 1497, he gave him a cloak ("una cappa") which cost no less than between twenty-five and thirty lire; there were eight yards of cloth in it, with green velvet for the facings, ribbons and I know not what. A note that casts a somewhat displeasing light on the young man's character follows the entry of this payment: "Salai rubò 4 soldi" (Salai has stolen four soldi).

In 1502, the kind-hearted Leonardo gave his pet retainer two gold ducats, to buy himself a pair of shoes trimmed with rose colour. He took an interest, too, in his favourite's family and lent him thirteen crowns, in 1508, to make up his sister's dowry.

In January 1505, Salai testified his great anxiety to "far qualche cosa galante", for the Marchesa Isabella d'Este. His offer does not seem to have been accepted and we are all the more astonished to find the Florentine correspondents of that lady selecting Leonardo's pupil to judge, nay, even to correct Perugino's picture, *The Battle between Love and Chastity*, which was to adorn the walls of the Palace at Mantua.

Salai accompanied Leonardo to Rome in 1514, but he refused to follow his master to France, preferring to settle in the house he built himself in the vineyard owned by the artist close to the gates of Milan. Leonardo, as we have seen, bequeathed half this vineyard to him. The later circumstances of Leonardo's favourite pupil and the date of his death are wrapped in obscurity.

The Superficial Anatomy of the Shoulder and Neck, c. 1510. Pen and ink with wash over charcoal lines, 28.9 x 19.8 cm. Royal Library, Windsor Castle.

No acknowledged work by Salai has yet been discovered, though a series of imitations, more or less free, of his master's works – the *Saint Anne*, the *Virgin and Child* in the Uffizi Gallery, the *Saint John* in the Ambrosiana – are ascribed to him. The *Holy Family* in the Brera, to which his name is affixed, is remarkable for its exceedingly intense, almost opaque, colour and for a general weakness, emptiness and lack of inspiration. The Virgin is of a pronounced Leonardesque type and the flowers that adorn the foreground are very carefully painted.

The two most brilliant disciples of the leader of the Milanese school, Antonio Bazzi, surnamed il Sodoma and Bernardino Luini, may never, possibly, have had the good fortune to listen to his counsels. I will give no fresh description in this place of the gifts of these two incomparable artists, nor of those of their successor, Gaudenzio Ferrari: my readers will allow me to refer them to the third volume of my *Histoire de l'Art pendant la Renaissance,* in which I have striven to make their work known and win both admiration and affection for it. I will only point out that the loving care, amounting to minute attention, which Leonardo lavished on the least of his productions, does not characterize either Luini or il Sodoma. Both these artists betray a tendency for generalization, without any recourse to the endless research that has as much to do with science as with art. They do not, in fact, belong to the fifteenth century and they were able, thanks to the efforts of their glorious forerunner, to make free use of the formulae he had so laboriously acquired. There is something literary, too, in their genius. They are more fitted for the brilliant development of some given subject, than inclined to strive after the solution of a technical problem, the rendering of some effect of light, the defining of some physiognomy, or characteristic object. In a word, there is as much of the poet in them as of the painter.

Portrait painting holds quite a secondary position in their artistic work, for they looked upon individual men and women merely as actors in their skilfully conceived and eloquently rendered scenes. They have none of the eager and untiring curiosity of their master.

Is it a fact that the Venetian school, in spite of much apparent affinity, never felt the effect of Leonardo's influence? It has been asserted that neither in Giorgione's work nor in that of Lorenzo Lotto, who has been occasionally described as one of the pupils of the leader of the Milanese school, can the slightest trace of any of Leonardo's teaching be discovered. As far as Giorgione is concerned, at all events, I have already demonstrated that his familiarity with Leonardo's work and tendencies was far greater than has been believed.

Titian's *Tribute Money* has appeared to several modern critics to attempt the same problems as the *Last Supper* in the Refectory of Sta Maria delle Grazie.

The painters Francesco Napoletano and Girolamo Aliprandi represent the Kingdom of Naples in this connection. The former may be studied in the Pinacoteca di Brera in a Virgin seated and holding the Child, brown in color, after the style of Boltraffio. The Child's eyes are puffy, the expression of the Virgin is irresolute. The type, with its high chin, somewhat recalls that of Leonardo's drawing in the Uffizi. It also reminds us of the *Madonna Litta*. Francesco Napoletano seems to have settled very early in the sixteenth century at Valencia, in Spain and never to have left that country again. A set of *Scenes from the Life of the Virgin* (1506) in the Cathedral of Valencia, is of a pronounced Leonardesque character. As for Girolamo Alibrando, or Aliprandi, of Messina (1470-1524), he studied Leonardo with so much ardour for his *Presentation in the Temple* in the Duomo at Messina, that the picture was long ascribed to the master.

In the seventeenth century, Rubens studied Leonardo da Vinci's work with passionate eagerness and paid eloquent homage to the greatness of his genius. When he passed through Milan he made a drawing of the *Last Supper*. We also owe him the copy of the central group in the *Battle of Anghiari*. Rembrandt, too, laid Leonardo under contribution.

My readers will thus realize the number of directions in which the influence of Leonardo disseminated itself. And these without taking into account either Correggio, or his own immediate pupils and imitators – Salai, Boltraffio, Marco d'Oggione, Cesare da Sesto andrea Solario, Melzi, Bernardino Luini, il Sodoma and Gaudenzio Ferrari.

We learn from the old legend that a single drop of milk from Juno's breast produced the Milky Way. Thus one look from the great Leonardo has sufficed to fill Italy and all Europe with masterpieces. Everywhere the seed sown by this mighty magician has brought forth fruit a hundredfold.

The Babe in the Womb,
c. 1510-1512.
Pen and ink with wash over red
chalk, 30 x 21.5 cm.
Royal Library, Windsor Castle.

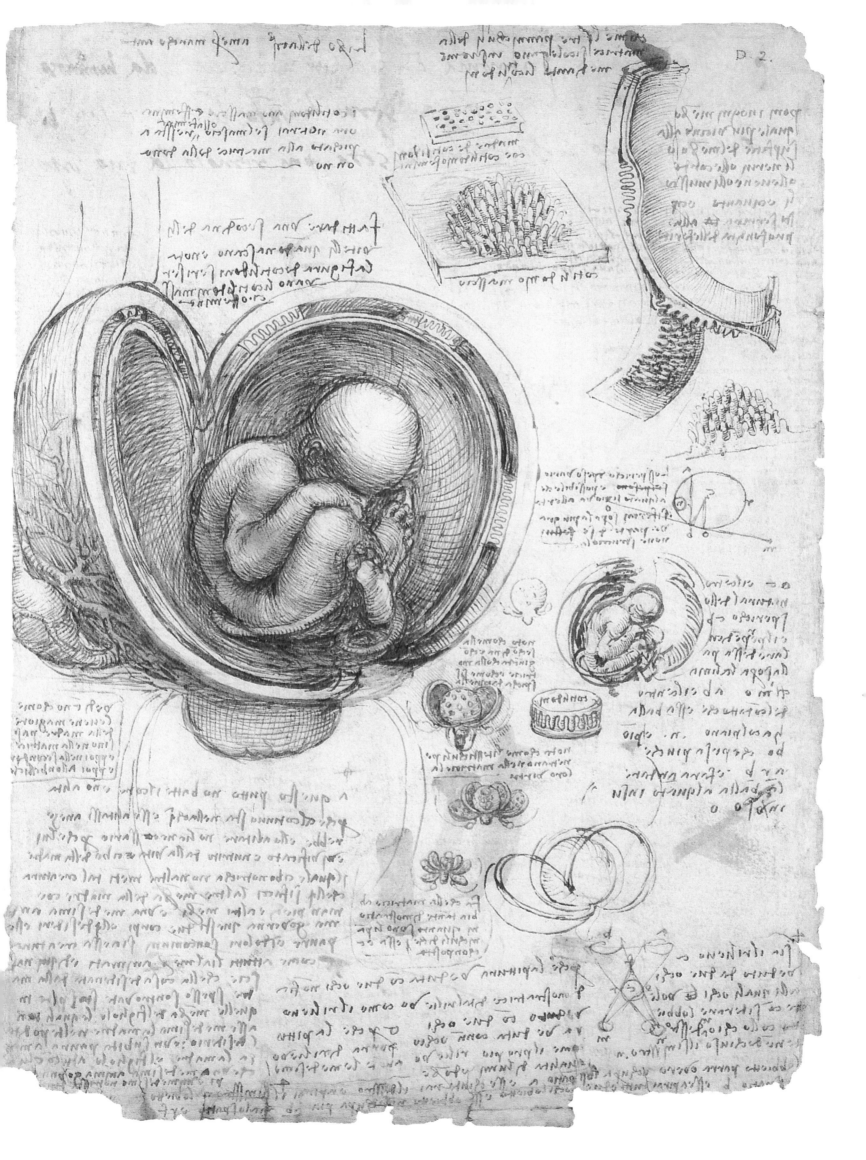

BIOGRAPHY

1452:

Leonardo is born on April 15th in a small Tuscan town called Anchiano near Vinci in the Florentine region. He is the illegitimate son of a wealthy notary, Ser Piero and a peasant girl, Caterina. His father takes charge of him after his birth, while Caterina leaves to marry another man. His two parents, each of them remarrying, give him seventeen brothers and sisters.

1457:

Leonardo goes to live with his father, who had married Alberia Amadori.

1460:

The young man follows his father to Florence.

1469:

At the age of fifteen, he becomes an apprentice in the famous studio of Andrea del Verrocchio in Florence.

1472:

He enters the painters' guild.

1473:

Leonardo paints the first of his famous works, *La Valle dell'Arno*.

1478:

He receives an order for an altar panel for the Vecchio Palace, a project that is never completed.

1492:

Leonardo leaves Florence for Milan. He manages to enter the service of Ludovico Sforza, the Duke of Milan. He remains as an artist in the court of Milan for eighteen years.

1492:

Leonardo paints *The Virgin of the Rocks*. He also designs elaborate armaments, among them a tank and war vehicles, as well as submarines and other battle engines.

1492:

He draws remarkable plans for a flying machine.

1495:

Leonardo begins work on *The Last Supper*, in the refectory of Santa Maria delle Grazie. The work is finished in 1498.

1496:

Leonardo meets the mathematician, Luca Pacioli, with whom he studies the treatises of Euclid.

1499:

The invasion of Milan by the French drives Leonardo from the city. He goes to Mantua, then to Venice and finally to Friuli seeking employment.

1502:

Leonardo begins work as a military engineer for Caesar Borgia, Duke of Romagna, son of Pope Alexander VI and General-in-Chief of his army. He supervises the building sites of the fortresses erected on the pontifical territories in central Italy.

1503:

He becomes a member of the commission charged with finding a place worthy of the statue *David* by Michelangelo. His talents as an engineer are in great demand during the war against Pisa. He draws sketches for *The Battle of Anghiari*.

1504:

His father dies on 9 July. There is a large inheritance, but Leonardo is swindled out of his share by the deception and trickery of his siblings. It is during this period that he begins to paint the *Mona Lisa*.

1506:

He returns to Milan at the request of the French Governor, Charles d'Amboise. There he passionately studies the four elements, earth, air, water and fire.

1507:

Leonardo is named painter of the court of Louis XII of France.

1514:

The artist returns to Rome where he comes under the patronage of Pope Leo X. He is heavily inclined toward scientific discoveries. However, his fascination for anatomy and physiology is hindered by the Pope's insistence that he should not open corpses for study purposes.

1516:

Leonardo's sponsor, Julio de' Medici, dies on 4 March. He is then invited to France to enter the service of Francis I, as First Painter, Engineer and Architect to the King.

1519:

Leonardo da Vinci dies on 2 May at Cloux and is buried in the church of Saint Valentine in Amboise. He leaves all of his manuscripts, drawings and tools to his favourite student, Francesco Melzi. All of the paintings remaining in his studio, including *Mona Lisa*, are given to Salai, another student.

LIST OF ILLUSTRATIONS

Leonardo